Corporate America's Final Solution

by

D.A. Robinson

authorHOUSE®

AuthorHouse™
1663 Liberty Drive, Suite 200
Bloomington, IN 47403
www.authorhouse.com
Phone: 1-800-839-8640

First published by AuthorHouse 4/17/2008

ISBN: 978-1-4343-7949-8 (sc)

*Printed in the United States of America
Bloomington, Indiana*

This book is printed on acid-free paper.

Introduction

All my life I've been extremely interested in American politics, almost to the point of it becoming an obsession. My main interests have always been centered on the social and economic trends brought about by the actions or in-actions of private, state and federal government. Being fifty-nine years old, going on sixty, I believe that I can safely say that I was born and grew up during the early years of what can now only be described as a very slowly evolving destructive trend, a trend fueled by American corporate policies that today have completely changed not only the quality of life for the majority of working Americans but have also greatly diminished the power of our United States Constitution, all done in order to enable American corporate powers to reach their intended goal. Our Constitution, the very document that America's founding fathers ratified in 1789, making it the foundation of our nation's democratic form of government and the basis for the social and economic freedoms that have caused our nation to stand apart from all others, freedoms which for millions of people living in those times were still yet unknown. That one most-important document penned in what I believe was an honest, sincere, and compassionate attempt by its creators to provide a fair and just political, economic, and legal system, a system from which a new and much more prosperous way of life for all the citizens of a new nation could grow. Little did our founding fathers realize that their actions would eventually bring about the creation of a society that can only be described as the greatest social experiment, the world has ever known.

I've learned many things during my life, some through formal education and observation and others through what sometimes amounted to very unforgettable and painful experiences, always brought about by my overwhelming desire to apply the trial and error method. Rather than listening to the sound and logical advice of older and wiser individuals, like my parents. I used to be the kind of guy who'd buy the kids a new swing set but never looked at the directions until I ended up holding what I always tried to make myself believe were leftover spare parts.

One lesson I learned well before reaching voting age was the fact that very few occurrences in life are ever as they first appear and most are never completely accidental. I'll even go a bit further by saying that aside from half of one percent, I'll give them at least that much. Nothing in the realm of political decision making is ever as it outwardly appears. Ninety nine point nine plus that left over half a percentile I mentioned concerning all actions

taken or not taken by government in the way of legislation passed or enforcement or lack of enforcement of
such legislation. Always has been, is, and will continue
to occur because of unseen and very calculated ulterior
motives. And each is designed to achieve some desired
effect or end, an end seldom if ever realized by the average man or woman on the street. Why, because you and
I are outside the political loop. In other words, we're not
privy to the reasoning behind such decisions. If we were,
more times than not, we'd probably be appalled and in
some cases, the occasionally used quote from an old spy
thriller "If I told you, I'd have to kill you," could very
well apply.

After reading my observations and conclusions you
may disagree with some or maybe even all. But if the
following pages provide the catalyst needed to cause you
the reader to ask your representatives why and finally
demand answers and true accountability from those we
elect to political office, then I've accomplished what I've
set out to do.

Before we the people can have effective, positive action designed to solve our nation's most serious political, social, and economic problems, we first have to ana-
lyze and then find the root cause of these problems, the
majority of which I sincerely believe were, are, and will
continue to be created by a government that today is
completely controlled by corporate powers and as such,
totally unresponsive to the needs of America's working
class majority. Many of my conclusions may appear outrageous, and even I have to admit that many of them are.
But when you consider that those whom we have elected

to protect our nation's security and our way of life are the very same individuals who for years have time and time again passed legislation that has shown a complete disregard for the welfare of America and the American people, while at the same time continually passing bills that favor the interests of large national and international corporations. To make even more clear the extent of their complicity in America's present-day situation, these same representatives of the people have time and time again offered up more and more of America's nuclear weapons technology, manufacturing base, and infrastructure for sale, and to of all people, the very same governments or government-controlled companies who are presently supporting, or at one time or another have supported, the terrorist organizations who seek to destroy us. These senators, congressmen, and yes, even past and present administrations have steadfastly stood by a continuing policy which more times than not ends in the awarding of contracts that simply put, have time and time again handed over control of a number of our seaports to the very nations I mentioned above; Nations, who in the past have been proven to financially support terrorist organizations whose only goal is the destruction of our country. When these same so called representatives of the people have already sold or voted in favor of the sale of numerous large enterprises that make up our nation's manufacturing base. How can we possibly believe that there are any limits to what they are capable of doing?

Corporate America's Final Solution is not just a compilation of my own personal, sometimes wandering and repetitious observations, thoughts, and predictions, all bound into book form. It's also a story about America's future and the future of our society, and maybe, just maybe, it's also a final warning. Whether it's one or all of the above, the fact remains that it is a story I felt I had to tell. Not just my story, but yours too.

Table of Contents

CHAPTER ONE

The Beginnings of Hope and the Gradual Decline there of

What I believe we are seeing in America today is simply the natural progression of what can only be described as an endless series of events all designed to maximize profits and strengthen corporate America's financial position, prior to and now in the new and fast-growing global economy, through the domination and eventual elimination of America's middle class and fair labor market. These events have all been allowed, no, encouraged to come about with the complete support of Federal and state government, in a country where today's working-class majority has absolutely no representation or voice in the critical decisions that so greatly affect our every day lives. Today's government more than at any other time in this nation's history exists for one purpose and one purpose only: to carry out corporate America's profit-orientated policies.

In order to understand the reasons for our present labor, wage, and increasingly deteriorating standard of living situation, I believe we must first look back in time to the beginning, when America first entered the mechanized age and the path that gradually led us to become the most powerful industrialized nation on earth.

During the late 1800s and early 1900s, wages and working conditions had deteriorated to a point where a great many of the working class believed that the only way to obtain decent wages and working standards was through uniting or banding together. Since companies could not be trusted to deal fairly with their employees, only through some sort of united labor force, or as it was eventually called, a labor union, could employees expect to have any meaningful leverage when, dealing with their employers. Because of this, in 1903 the International Brotherhood of Teamsters, Chauffeurs, Warehousemen, and helpers were founded. In the years that followed it became known as The Teamsters Union, or more commonly, the Teamsters.

As the years of tremendous change and sometimes violent conflicts passed, the Teamsters membership grew, and with it, so did its power. During this period, unions representing all types of trades and occupations sprang up throughout our country, and every labor union, even those not affiliated with the Teamsters, benefited from the bargaining power and record achieved by the leaders of the Teamster membership. America was now very quickly becoming a unionized nation. The union president who led the Teamsters at the pinnacle of their power was a man named James Hoffa. Under his leadership, wages and working conditions along with the union employee's standard of living improved dramatically. For the first time in our nation's history, a noticeable segment of America's working-class population began to realize that their hopes and dreams for a brighter tomorrow were more than just that. They could actually become a reality. Americans, many for the first time, not only owned a single automobile but were now buying a second car for the wife and even taking vacations that for the average family of the time had been thought impossible to even consider. Some bought winter homes or fishing cabins in the mountains. Many families now found themselves in a position to offer their children the opportunity of building a better life for themselves through higher education. The American dream was alive! It was real! It was here, in a place that was surely the land of opportunity. In America, a person could be what he or she wanted to be. It wasn't easy, especially for women of the time who were involved in their own struggle for equality, a struggle that to some degree still exists today. But it still could happen. Oh, it took work and lots of it, hard work, persistence, and dedication.

But that was about to change. Because of Jimmy Hoffa and men like him, corporate America's dominance and control in the workplace, along with record-breaking, seemingly limitless profits were now being threatened. These profits, which had been the yearly norm, were now slipping away. They had to fight back. They had to regain control, but how? I believe the war on the working people of America began as a slight, unnoticeable ripple, around the time James Hoffa was sent to prison. I'm not saying that Mr. Hoffa's sentencing was the, or for that matter, even "a" factor in what someone who's a bit paranoid might conclude to be step one of a master plan, but that the down hill slide for the American worker appeared to begin ever so slowly a short time later.

But just for the sake of argument, let's get paranoid for a moment and take a step far outside the realm of believability. Let's ask a seemingly absurd question: Could it even be remotely possible that the removal of the most powerful union leader this nation has ever seen was indeed the first step in a long series of corporate schemes, strategies, or whatever term one might use. Strategies that have been able to successfully bring about the situation that America's middle class now faces? A plan, or maybe more accurately stated, a series of policies, each designed to eventually enable America's corporate powers to achieve the greatest percentage of profit possible, a long-term scheme created by the highest echelons of America's most powerful corporations. The invisible few, the real power behind the power, or if you'd like, the individuals who truly hold in their hands the reigns that control Capitol Hill, the White House, and along with it, the destinies of us all. If indeed true, it would be a plan that in order for it to succeed would have to include the eventual destruction of America's middle class, and along with it, a standard of living that millions of us have enjoyed for decades.

Right now, you're probably saying to yourself, another outrageous conspiracy theory, and maybe you're right. Maybe I've become caught up in what appears to be the most serious problem ever faced, not only by today's middle class Americans, but also by America itself. A kind of growing mass frustration and distrust of government brought on by the stark realization of just how enormous and far reaching the level of corruption truly is. This knowledge kept alive in the minds of all of us by the intense media coverage. News stories for years that have been aimed directly at allegations of massive widespread government corruption, corruption that appears to becoming more and more prevalent with each passing day.

But wait, wait just a minute. If you were to set the farfetched possibility of a long range corporate conspiracy alongside one or two other very old stories of which admittedly there have seen several variations. The majority, appearing to have been based quite a bit more on fact than fabrication. Then maybe the possibility I've presented here might not appear so outlandish. The first of these two stories involves an organization founded somewhere around the tenth century BC. Today, they are known as the masons, a self described fraternal organization somewhat involved in charity work. The masons of today were originally known as the free Stone Masons. The word "free" included in their title referred to their ability to travel freely throughout Europe to wherever their work took them. This authority was given to all free masons at a time in history when the average person or peasant's travel was greatly restricted. The members of the free masons although uneducated and illiterate were said to have possessed divine god given knowledge and powers which enabled them to build elaborate, stone structures. Many of which were cathedrals. All their work accomplished using just a few basic tools such as a compass, an ancient version of the level, and stone chisels. History credits the stone masons with the building of Solomon's temple, approximately one thousand years before the birth of Christ. History also tells us that during the crusades. Seven knights were sent from France in order to protect the population of Christian pilgrims who were living in the Middle East at the time. Upon their arrival in Jerusalem the knights were housed in a building that was said to have been built on top of the ruins of Solomon's temple. Built by King Herod, whose purpose it was to replace the temple with one of his own design. The name Knights Templar or protector of the temple was given to the seven knights who were housed in that building. Throughout the centuries that followed. The paths and fortunes of the free Masons and the Knights templar appear to be intertwined. Is it possible that the free masons along with the Knights templar were the actual founders of the Masonic Order?

The Templar, now growing in numbers, and having numerous duties to perform, one of which involved the loaning of money and the security and transportation of huge amounts of wealth between the Middle East and Europe, became tremendously wealthy. This fact alone is quite interesting considering that from what I've read, the Nights Templar originally swore an oath of poverty.

As the years passed, the fortunes these men were able to amass was said to have been so great that even a king and a pope found themselves unable to resist their desire to confiscate it. So, two powerful leaders, Pope Clement the V, and King Philip the IV of France, after conspiring together, sent their agents out during the early morning hours of October 13, 1307. Hundreds of templar were arrested, tried and tortured before being burned at the state. Being able to confiscate the fortunes of one or even large numbers of individuals wasn't an exceptionally hard task. Not when you consider the immense power held by the Roman Catholic Church during that period. A charge of heresy and/or treason was easily obtained, and sufficient enough grounds to demand the sentence of death. Those Masons who were fortunate enough to elude capture fled Europe to the safety of several other countries. Years later, many of their descendants migrated to the new world, America.

Through the years I've read historical accounts and I've watched documentaries that have linked the Masonic Order to certain events or happenings in our country's history. One curious event concerns the creation of a pyramid containing what is referred to as the "all-seeing eye," the one found on our dollar bill. It's also been written that some of the signers of the Declaration of Independence were members of the Masonic order, even presidents. Till this day, it is still unknown how great a part the Masons played, if any, in past or present-day America. Why, because of the secrecy surrounding the Masonic order. No one today actually knows the deepest innermost workings of the Order of Masons. One thing is for sure. The story of the free Stone Masons and the Knights Templar is, if I say so myself, pretty incredible. And maybe, just maybe, if you think about it for a minute or two, you might find that it makes my speculations concerning Hoffa and the plausibility of corporate America's long-range plan, appear just a little more conceivable.

Let's continue but more briefly along the same lines by discussing another organization referred to as the Skull and Bones. From what I understand it was started sometime during the late 1800s at Harvard University and is still active today. A number of extremely powerful corporate heads, successful politicians, and past American presidents have been members of this secretive organization. But instead of discussing the Skull and Bones to any great length, I'll just say that among these members are the most wealthy and most powerful people in this country. And they all have a couple of things in common. Besides the ability to be able to build upon the wealth they already have. It appears that they have the knack of achieving government and corporate positions that have continually given these individuals the ability to create, dictate and control America's national and international political and economic policies. Decisions that lead to the creation of these policies eventually determine the direction of corporate investment and return on such investments. The power held by these individuals is not limited to within the borders of the United States, but reaches throughout the world, and like the Masonic order, just how deeply involved the Skull and Bones fraternity is in American and world affairs will never truly be known. Why, because every member takes his oath of secrecy very seriously. Not one past or present member who is or has been considered a credible source has ever given any in-depth information concerning the organization. After completing my investigation of these organizations, I find myself asking three very intriguing questions. Number one, is there any connection between the Knights Templar, the free Masons, the skull and bones and the situation America faces today? Number two; are these all just individual and for the most part, fraternal organizations? And number three; how many of today's leader's, belong to all three?

I guess we can always discount the possibility of a series of secretive corporate policies. We can write any thought of them off as being pure speculation, or maybe, consider what I've proposed as no more than a plausible outline for a good or not-so-good fiction novel. Yes, we could push the thought aside in favor of good ole basic common sense. Funny thing about perception, common sense and logic—we all have a different version of. What's logical to me could very well be considered illogical to someone else. Two people can look at the same robbery suspect, and not see the same person. When we see black, there's always someone in the same room who will argue that we're actually looking at white. Californians have proven time and time again that for many of their residents, there's no limit to the number of variations or perceptions of all three. Ever since the O. J. Simpson verdict and the court decision concerning the poor guy who was hit in the head repeatedly with bricks, I've come to the conclusion that California residents have a completely different mindset when it comes to logical thought processes, not to mention justice. Who knows, maybe it's the water. That or the funny looking plants they grow in their basements.

If we were to disregard the possibility I mentioned above. I guess we'd have to accept the fact that everything that's transpired in the workplace during the last one hundred-plus years has simply been an accident, or coincidence. Or I suppose we could attribute America's present social and economic situation as simply a natural progression of events, each driven by one of man's strongest and most basic traits. I'm referring of course to greed.

I realize full well that my assessments regarding this nation's current situation not to mention my predictions for its future. Are as I stated above, for the most part purely speculation. A series of conclusions that I've reached after weeks, months, and years as a guy on the street, an average American who has been observing government and how it relates to business and visa versa, ever since I was a teen. I'd like to return for a moment in order to end my previous discussion of the Hoffa trial by saying that at the conclusion of the United States vs. James Hoffa, on that day, the front page of every newspaper across this country had the story. "Hoffa sentenced". And that wasn't speculation. They had the story all right. They had it on page one. But did they have the real story? Why was Jimmy Hoffa sent to prison? Since that day, our history books have told the story of a corrupt union leader, a man who aligned himself with the mafia. But anyone who has read a number of books dedicated to the preservation of history knows that quite a bit of it is much closer to being fiction than actual historical fact. Here however is a fact you can take to the bank. Back in the 1930s in cities like Chicago and New York, it was very hard to tell the difference between the government and the local mob.

Why was James Hoff imprisoned? Was it because he broke the law or was it because he had become too powerful? Had he foolishly led the working-class people of America across that invisible line, the line that has always separated those who have from those who have not? For one moment, let's take a very short look at the man who led the federal prosecution of Mr. Hoffa. His name was Robert Kennedy, brother of then-president John F. Kennedy. Considering the upper financial end or segment of American society that Robert Kennedy occupied, I find it easier to believe that his allegiance lay not with the American working people or the Internal Revenue Service, but rather with America's corporate powers. Why did Kennedy pull out all the stops? What was the real force behind his tremendous drive to get Hoffa? What was his true motivation?

During the years that followed. The changes happening in the American workplace were very low-key, very subtle. So much that for the average worker they were hardly if ever noticed and even if noticed, the reasons behind these changes appeared so remote and innocent that they were never connected. But as some of us learned years later, many companies, using covert practices, had set up bank accounts that were created and used for one purpose and one purpose only, to manipulate union officials in order to gain the upper hand when negotiating contracts. Their ability to control many of these unions was accomplished through job appointments, gifts, trips, and untraceable cash. As the years went by, companies aided by corrupt union officials and a court system that without reservation turned their heads began a series of cost-cutting measures that time and time again violated union agreements. All these measures were designed to increase corporate profits, sometimes at the expense of the quality of their products and always at the expense of the American worker. Any who complained were told what I was once told by the shop steward of the union I belonged to: "You're lucky you have a job."

As ridiculous as it may seem, I believe that the creation of salaried employees was one of their small, hardly noticeable, but successful—how should I put it—ways of testing the waters. During these years and most always supported by the federal government, they stepped up their anti-union practices by publicly chipping away at union contracts, which in most cases usually resulted in wage and benefit reductions. Again, in open violation of union contracts, companies began buying steel and other materials needed to produce their own finished products. Not from their traditional U.S. suppliers, but from Japan, China, and a short list of third-world nations. As a result, a ripple effect was felt throughout the American manufacturing community. America's steel industry and the American suppliers of raw materials that depended upon the steel industry for their very existence began to fail.

What was about to happen wasn't something new. It was just a much, much smaller new and improved version of the Depression of 1929. The driving force or motivation behind each of these events was and always will be the same: greed, money, and power. Greed is the motivating factor that drives you to obtain the money. Once you have the money, the power always follows. This being the case, there is no doubt in my mind that the never-ending drive to acquire both is also the same motivating factor behind the creation of a global economy and America's current social and economic situation. And since man is as he is and always will be. His desire to obtain these all-important commodities will always provide the incentive necessary to create any number of similar events in the future.

Manipulating the marketplace in order to force smaller, less solvent companies into bankruptcy is the business world's version of what most of us know as "the law of the jungle." Instead of physically devouring one's victims, the financially stronger companies, sometimes for pennies or less on the dollar, devour the smaller, weaker ones. How should I phrase this so as not to upset America's industrial headhunters? As if I really give a damn. I suppose I could use one of their descriptions like corporate reorganization or downsizing. How about absorption? Hmm, a slight modification process sounds rather unthreatening.

Have you ever noticed that in America we always use such nice words to describe horrific events? Mugging is one of my favorites. Whenever I hear the word mug or mugging I think about sitting in front of a nice warm fire on a cold winter night, sipping on a hot cup of cocoa, not a man, woman, or child being beaten so badly that they will never be the same again. Well, corporate America's descriptions of what they do in order to achieve maximum profits are similar in that they never even come close to describing the horrendous effects their cost-cutting policies have on employees and their families. As every working American knows, each and every one of these terms, when applied, always means the loss of jobs or a reduction in wages, benefits or all three. For many Americans, it means much more than the end of their jobs, or the end of their careers. Because no matter how you label it, no matter how much sugar coating is applied, the loss of one's job also means quite possibly the eventual destruction of the family unit and the lives of those who make up those family units. It means the end of a way of life for all those who are unfortunate enough to be on the receiving end of a company's drive for higher profits.

During the mini-depression I described, job losses were pretty much kept to a minimum. So at the time, unemployment never became a large upfront issue, an issue that corporate America couldn't afford to face head on, at least not at the time.

Once again, corporate America's law of the jungle prevailed and the strong survived. But even before the dust had completely settled, the survivors began using their increased financial power to continue expanding their operations by acquiring more and more of the companies who were forced into bankruptcy. All these numerous new acquisitions by the survivors eventually led to the creation of something that at one time in this country was considered totally illegal. But now, for reasons known only to lobbyists, corporate board members, and the politicians who were and still are owned by corporate power, they are not. I'm referring to a "monopoly." Its birth, or better said, its rebirth coupled with the so-called new global economy would soon change the lives of every working American. Some would find their lot improving. But for the vast majority, their wages, benefits, and standard of living would continue to slowly decline. Corporate America, especially now, under this country's Bush administration, is completely unhindered by the federal regulations and laws that once prevented the existence of monopolies. Because these laws are now ignored, corporate powers are free to create the monsters that have not only become a fact of life in America but also the greatest, most destructive threat this nation's working class has ever seen. Corporate America's new and ever-growing financial strength now magnified many times over has enabled these new corporate gargantuans to buy up and/or control the industries that are in effect the lifeblood of our nation's working people; examples of which are the oil, gas, electric, health, and pharmaceutical industries. These newly formed huge American powerbrokers continued to gradually reduce their reliance on the American workforce by signing contracts with foreign companies to produce the products Americans used to make. Oh, in most cases the products sold in the United States still carried the brand names of American companies but were not made in America or by American labor.

My first encounter with imported goods occurred when I was a seven-year-old kid, back in the mid-50s. At the time a small number of American companies began importing stamped metal toys from Japan. These toys on our store shelves were viewed by most people as a novelty. The American consumer, myself included, had no idea what significance that little stamped metal toy had. We had no idea just how far corporate America was planning to take their new policies concerning the importation of foreign-made goods.

Through the years, because of the ever-increasing amount of merchandise we have imported and continue to import, as well as the unlimited scope of the products introduced into our economy, we have now become a nation subservient to the newest and greatest industrial power on Earth: China. Let's face it: We are almost totally dependent on imports for our own survival. How did it happen? How did America fall from being the most modern and industrialized nation in the world? The answer is quite simple. Corporate America's never-ending quest for more and cheaper products has for the most part destroyed our nation's manufacturing base. After only a short few years as an industrialized nation, China not only passed Japan to take over the number one spot as our largest trading partner. They; blew their doors off. For decades now the shelves in our stores have been piled high with every imaginable product, and since all of us red-blooded Americans love a deal, we bought big. And we still do. Why? Hell, any idiot can tell you why—because the price was right. But was it? Was it really? By now, I think a great majority of Americans have come to realize that the cost was far too high.

The problems we face today concerning the flood of imports, presents all of us with a few tough questions. How can we go back? And will corporate America ever allow it? Will the people who reside on Capitol Hill and in the White House create and pass legislation that will allow America to return to being a nation of strength and independence, a country free from being controlled by nations like China, Japan, and Saudi Arabia? Will America ever return to being the America we older folks grew up in? The nation many of us served and many thousands of others gave their lives for?

If not, if our course is set in stone and unchangeable, if we allow corporate America to decide our future, then all we can look forward to is a continuing decline in the way we live and eventually not only the end of America but the end of our freedom and the end of the dream our forefathers called democracy.

Ninety-nine percent of all the goods we buy today, in order to maintain our way of life, are imported, including the majority of the fruits and vegetables we eat. Chicken, fish, shrimp, flatware, clothes, dog food, even a large percentage of the automobiles we drive, are imported. The list is endless, and as far as U.S. carmakers' claims of being "made in America," even that's false. Years ago, our, excuse me, their legislators passed a law stating that before any auto manufacturer could claim that their car was American made, it had to be at least seventy five percent made in America. What ever happened to one hundred percent? Let's get technical for a second. Does that mean made, or assembled? Have you ever noticed the words made in Mexico or Canada on the windshield of your Ford Taurus? Don't be surprised if it says Mexico, China, Japan etc., etc. Everywhere except America.

Yes, just about everything we buy today is made somewhere else. Think about that and ask yourself this question. Where did the American workers go? Where are the American workers who used to make that hairbrush, dish, knife and fork, and every product we use in our everyday lives? Don't forget the windshield in your

Taurus. We're not looking at a couple of million jobs lost. I can truthfully say that because American companies have been importing foreign goods, exporting American jobs, and importing cheap labor for so many years, an accurate tallying of lost jobs would be extremely difficult to arrive at. But I assure you, it's much, much greater a number than any U.S. government survey would admit to. There's one very important thing that Americans have apparently forgotten, something I've found to be so very true. Whether we're talking about your job seniority in relationship to the number of people you have under you or the number of people being laid off anywhere in America, sooner or later, what affects those living and working hundreds or even thousands of miles away could very well affect you, even if there's no apparent connection.

One of our most famous presidents once said, "United we stand, divided we fall." The gentleman's name was Abraham Lincoln, and he was referring to the secession of the southern states from the Union. That statement not only applies to the states that make up this nation; it also applies to all people everywhere who are engaged in a struggle of any kind, including the struggle that every working American faces today. With government-supported destruction of America's unions and Washington's steadfast policy of looking the other way on illegal immigration and border security, with corporate-created business deals not only supported but heavily pushed by U.S. government trade agreements, we are now more than ever dependent on foreign goods and services. Our dependence on these imports has not only created the labor situation we are now faced with, but in doing so, the past and present Washington administrations have also successfully destroyed the level of security our country, any country, must have and maintain in order to survive as a sovereign nation.

Millions of people, mostly from Mexico, have for years been able to simply climb over a fence or in many cases just walk across our border and automatically become entitled to free education, medical care, and some sort of Social Security benefit or benefits. Let's not forget the states that hand out driver's licenses and food stamps to people who are not supposed to be in this country in the first place. When referring to Social Security, I'm talking about benefits that in most cases Americans have had to work for years before becoming eligible to even apply for, or as calculated by the Social Security administration, so many quarters.

Corporate America's ability to obtain the support of the Supreme Court and the people we elect to represent us has resulted in our complete loss of representation in Washington. At this point in time we no longer have "anyone" in Washington whose job it is to safeguard and protect our way of life, no one to honestly protect us against the very same forces that James Hoffa and people like him had to confront just after the turn of the twentieth century.

Are we on the path of regression, to the days of the sweat shops, to unlimited work hours, without a decent wage, to a time in our nation's history when the American worker was treated as less than human, a time when workers had no rights at all in the workplace? Are the years of the Great Depression of 1929 returning? A period in America's not-so-glorious past when crowds of people formed outside factories in the early morning darkness, waiting, hoping, and praying that the company lackey would choose them just for one day's work? A time when shanty towns lined the railroad tracks of this country? When local police set up barricades outside towns in order to keep transients out? Those transients were our grandparents and great-grandparents. Those transients were Americans who had not only lost their jobs and their homes, but for many, had lost any hope of ever seeing the light at the end of what appeared to be an endless black tunnel. For a vast majority of these people, there was no hope, and no tomorrow. Is that America's future? Believe me, if, or maybe better said, when another Depression similar to 1929 does return, it will be far worse. The questions I just presented are questions that all of us had better think about and better fear. Can't happen! In order to answer that, I'll use a quotation from another time. "Those who fail to learn from the past are doomed to repeat the past." It's a proven fact that history does repeat itself, and here's one more fact that life has taught me. It goes like this. For the average man or woman who punches a clock, for people like you and I who live pretty much from paycheck to paycheck, life never stays the same. For us, life is not a constant. It's always changing. Our lives are filled with ups and downs. Good times and lean times and holding onto those good times have become more and more difficult with the passage of time.

I was born about fourteen years after the Great Depression, but even as an eight-year-old kid, I still remember a couple of the stories my mother told me. I remember her talking about how my father and his brothers had to walk the railroad tracks that ran along the Hudson river in South Troy, New York, picking up chunks of coal that they would later burn in the kitchen stove so they'd have some sort of heat when night came. I remember her telling me about how my dad's father, my grandfather, used to get the meat and potatoes at dinner time. That is, if they were fortunate enough to have meat. And as for the rest of the family, they ate bread soaked in gravy. She told me how he kicked my father down the stairs when he told him he wanted to stay in school. His old man screamed at him to get his ass out and find a job. For years, even after his death, I hated my grandfather for what he'd done. But now I'm too old to hate and I guess if you considered just how very hard life was during the depression years. Maybe just as I have, you too will be able to understand the reason why his old man did what he did. Whatever the case, cruel or not, I'm not the one to judge him. In those days, for thousands of families, every cent that came into the house was pooled. The money wasn't being saved for a rainy day or a vacation. It wasn't being put aside for that new big-screen TV. It was about eating today and tomorrow and the day after. It was about staying warm. It was about survival. For all those who know nothing of those years, all I can say is that from the stories I remember, living through them can only be described as hell on Earth.

There are several reasons why I sincerely believe that the majority of today's Americans would be unable to survive a serious Depression. (1) America's population has grown tremendously since 1929, from approximately

122 million to 281.5 million in the year 2000. With the heavy influx of illegal aliens during the last eight years alone and the number who were never included in the last census, the actual population could be twenty or thirty million plus higher than the 2000 census. (2) The number of family-owned and company-owned farms that existed in this country during those years has been significantly reduced. In their place we now find factories, some of whose doors have closed, malls, condominiums, golf courses, and gated communities, just to name a few. The end result of all this construction or maybe a better word would be destruction comes to us in the form of a considerable reduction in usable farmland. Scientists, realizing the probability and seriousness of a situation that would eventually result in future food shortages, have been developing and constantly testing new ways to improve crop yield. But as hard as they try, their efforts will probable never result in their being able to produce enough food to support our entire nation. (3) Because America's manufacturing base has been pretty much destroyed, I might add, at a hefty profit to corporate America. I find myself wondering how many millions of Americans would be out of work and unable to buy the things they needed to survive? (4) We are, as I mentioned before, now almost totally dependent upon foreign countries, including our enemies, for our survival. (5) The last several generations growing up in America were never taught or for some reason have never learned the resourcefulness of their ancestors.

My father died when I was eight, leaving my mother to raise me alone. I'll never know how she did it. But she kept a roof over my head and kept me clothed and there was always food on the table. Not just food, but good food, delicious food. She kept the house in repair by taking nickels and stretching them into dollars. She went without and I never knew it. She took one meal and made four, all this by being extremely resourceful and working her fingers to the bone in a sweatshop shirt factory on River Street in Troy, New York. Being a kid, I never realized how hard it was for my mother. She never asked for help from anyone, and she never complained. And now, as I near the end of my life, I realize more fully the struggle and hardship she must have endured. The reason I included that very small piece of my own personnel history is because I wanted to give you the reader a little insight into the difference between the men and women then and now.

In those days, parents did what they had to do. There was no running away. The vast majority of parents were there for the duration. Think for a moment. Remember the marriage vows that you and the love of your life exchanged at the church alter? Words that went something like this: In sickness and in health, for richer or poorer, until death do us part? I hate to say this, but I truly believe that people, especially the young people of today, lack the strength and discipline necessary to enabled them to survive a 1929 and the lean years that would inevitably follow. My mother and people like her were from a different time. They were from a generation of determined, disciplined people, men and women who knew hardship. Hardship, at least to some degree and for most, was a way of life, so much so that they never thought of it as being hardship. They thought of it as life. All those past generations of men and women who came before us.

Americans who built this once great and true nation are now gone, and in their place we have a generation who've never experienced anywhere near the degree of hardship and despair that accompanied the Great Depression. The resourcefulness, discipline, and determination that people like my parents and grandparents had. Qualities that made it possible for them to survive during a time of extreme adversity have vanished along with them. The reasons I've stated above, and a couple more that I failed to include cause me to believe that not if, but when another 1929 does arrive, the human and social devastation experienced by today's Americans will be far greater than that experienced by our ancestors. At this time, I'd like to make one comment. For anyone who doesn't know the difference between a recession and a depression, I'd like to clear that up by using my own definition. A recession always happens to someone else, like the family down the street. A depression, which is always many times worse, occurs when it happens to you. After all, it's always worse when it happens to you, right! As with all things in life, depressions and recessions all come in different sizes. But whatever the size, it is not and never has been an enjoyable experience.

CHAPTER TWO

Corporate Migration

The next step by American big business was designed to do a number of things, all resulting in of course, maximum profits. By establishing their own factories in places like China, Japan, Mexico, or third-world countries they could eliminate the costly need of operating and maintaining their plants here in the United States. For the companies involved, this meant they were now able to reduce operating expenses even further by increasing cuts in their American workforce, in some cases retaining just enough people to fill orders and process paperwork. Many company-owned buildings were turned into warehouses. Any unnecessary space was either dismantled, sold, rented, or leased. Other companies took downsizing to an even higher level by completely closing their plants and having orders sent from their newly established overseas facilities directly to the American buying public. By manufacturing their own goods in foreign countries rather than purchasing them from foreign-owned companies, they were able to completely eliminate the middleman, and because the weekly wage for workers in those countries was considerably less than the average day's pay for an American, the move meant a tremendous reduction in operating expenses and thus created higher profits.

One more tremendous plus for these corporate giants made the move even more inviting. Countries like China and Mexico had little or no regulations concerning pollution. This being the case, these companies were able to take advantage of that country's lack of regulation by dumping the by-products created during the manufacturing process of their products which in many cases, included toxic waste, into rivers and open and closed pits. Does this situation still exist today? There's no doubt in my mind that at least to some degree, it still does. The reason I feel comfortable with that statement lies in the fact that for years, the Mexican government's complete lack of concern for the health and welfare of its people has been common knowledge here in the United States. Across our western border, one of the major dumpsites for newly established, X-American companies was the conveniently located Rio Grande River. Because of this, as time passed, people living along that river began having health problems. Babies were being born with severe birth defects, and others died from exposure to the chemicals that were being dumped there.

But why should the companies who were responsible for creating this deadly health hazard care? It wasn't their problem. After all, they were operating within Mexico's laws. And of course, there was big business's old standby of hiring scientific teams whose investigations always resulted in findings favorable to the companies that hired them, ending with the company issuing a public statement that went something like this: After a complete and exhaustive investigation of this situation by an independent team, they've concluded that the waste being emitted by our facility into the Rio Grande has no connection what-so-ever with the current health problems of local citizens. Doesn't that sound an awful lot like a statement that's been echoed for years by big tobacco? The same one that's been so eagerly accepted by our, excuse me, their federal government? The U.S government instead of closing down big tobacco or outlawing cigarettes has fined them millions of dollars. Hell, they don't want to close them down. They're too great a source of added revenue. What they want to do is bleed them a little bit every now and then. What about the health of our young, not a problem, free will, remember?

Because big tobacco, as well as the American corporations that moved across the border into Mexico. The "we don't have anything to do with it" type of defense, supported by dozens of high-priced company lawyers, has always had the ability to tie up any case for years. In Mexico, a few well-placed contributions should have the same effect. Then again, maybe I've overlooked stories relating to the cleanup. But I can truthfully say that I have never read any article or articles that told of the Mexican government's attempts to clean up the Rio Grande pollution situation. So as far as I know, it still exists.

A person who's inclined to be a bit sarcastic could say that the problem still exists because money is power and since the peasants living along the river are quite a bit more than just poverty stricken. They lack the financial wherewithal necessary to hire attorneys or bribe the government officials who are overseeing the case. For these reasons and the reasons I previously stated, I have to believe that the pollution problem does and will continue to exist. Because of the Mexican government's lack of compassion for its poor and after years of reading about the corruption that thrives south of the border. It's not at all hard for me to believe in my conclusions regarding big business and Rio Grande dumpsite.

Now back to the good ole U.S.A. Still having millions of American workers on their payrolls, men and women whose continued employment still amounted to a substantial financial drain on corporate earnings, companies turned their attention once again to ridding themselves of many more of the people they no longer had any use for. With the federal and state governments standing on the sidelines and the power of the majority of the unions destroyed through various, sometimes dubious, not to mention illegal methods, only minor obstructions, if any, stood between companies and their quest for more and more by the big boys or heavy hitters who were growing bigger by the day. If there's one thing we all have to give corporate America credit for. It's their ability to be consistent. They never ever let up. The machines, that turn out these new and improved innovative downsizing plans run twenty-four/seven and never stop. Each plan, if successfully executed, will in time bring America's middle class to the point of extinction.

With the prospects of attaining even higher record-breaking profits, American companies immediately turned up the throttle on their policies of systematic downsizing, getting rid of, in many cases, two or three generations of family member who worked for these companies and were the very same people who through their years of hard work and long hours had created the prosperity these companies now enjoyed. For those who survived this current elimination of jobs, they could only look forward to further reductions not only in wages but also in other benefits such as retirement, paid vacations, sick days, and healthcare. Each and every time a union contract came due, talks involving employee medical coverage seemed to immediately come to the forefront of the negotiations and became more and more of a stumbling block, most times ending with health plans being cut or modified or becoming co-pay policies with ever-increasing amounts being paid by employees, or as in many cases, no health coverage at all. Other methods designed to eliminate employee benefits also became very popular, like hiring people as part-time help or limiting work hours to just below forty, so companies didn't have to pay certain additional benefits. The hiring of subcontractors has also added to a substantial reduction in operating expenses. By employing subs, a company could not only circumvent the minimum wage law, paying people even less, but all taxes and employee benefits became the sole responsibility of the subcontractor, and because of certain stipulations in contracts, the subcontractors could quite easily end up working many more hours without any additional pay. This, as I mentioned above, sidesteps that state's preset minimum wage.

One of the earliest and most overlooked money-saving methods used by the agricultural segment of corporate America was the use of illegal aliens in place of American farm workers. Since at the time, the American job market was still on the upswing and jobs were pretty easy for most of us to find, I guess we never realized that the use of illegal aliens would ever develop into the threat that it is today, and besides, how many Americans wanted to do the kind of backbreaking work associated with picking fruit and vegetables? At first, the influx of illegal aliens was just a trickle, just a few jobs here and there, mostly in the farming sector. But like any small leak in any huge dam, unless it is stopped, it can grow. And that's exactly what it did. That small, hardly noticeable trickle, thanks to politicians who have and still do create and pass legislation on state and federal levels, congressman and senators who in reality owe their allegiance to corporate America and not the American voters who gave them their jobs has now become a torrent. As I just mentioned, years ago, most migrant workers, illegal or not, worked in the fields. Now they work in factories, build houses, drive trucks, and do landscaping and many other jobs that average Americans used to do.

While visiting two theme parks in Florida, I couldn't help but notice that both have begun replacing American workers with non-Americans. As a matter a fact, while visiting one park, I doubt if I heard the English language more than a half a dozen times during the eight hours my family and I spent there.

So where did the Americans go? Well, if they haven't found new jobs, they're either standing in unemployment lines or have become members of a not-so-new but quickly growing segment of America, a population of Americans that I guess we might as well refer to as the invisible society. They're, or working for wages that are well below the poverty level.

Don't get me wrong. I can't blame the illegal immigrants for wanting a better way of life. I do, however, blame them for coming here illegally. I also place 99.9 percent of the blame on past and present Washington administrations that are in reality nothing less than the legislative, executive, and judicial branches of corporate America.

Hold on now! Before you disagree with me, take a good look around. Don't rely on the current administration's boast of a terrific economy. Whenever our current president discusses the economy, he's appraising it from the prospective of someone sitting behind a desk in the boardroom of one of America's top ten corporations. If corporate profits are breaking records, then the economy's doing great, and there's that good ole saying that's been echoed by so many CEOs for so many years: "What's good for corporate America is good for America, right, wrong!" In this day and age, a little honesty, even if we hated what the individual was saying, would be like a breath of fresh air. So why not just scrap all the bullshit and come up with one saying that tells it like it really is? You know, "THE TRUTH." I believe the saying I'm looking for was probably first heard in the boardroom of what has to be the most hated oil company in America today. Pretty much says it all: "Greed is good." Yes, I believe that covers it, and it also explains in a nutshell why America's middle class will some day in the not-too-distant future be reduced to a memory whose historical significance will be noted in a few lines found between the covers of volume sixteen or seventeen of the Funk and Wagnall's new encyclopedia or possibly a high school history book.

If a person were to sit down and really think about corporate America's plan for our future and how their policies have been instituted in the countries where they do business, it might more easily explain, at least to a great degree, why America's relationship with the rest of the world is as it is today. "Greed is good." Is it, especially when it's carried to the extreme, as it is, here in America and abroad? When is enough, enough? Everything in life has a price. Unfortunately, when it comes to the policies that have been created by corporate America, the middle class and the poor always pay that price.

Years ago, if American companies prospered, then American workers prospered. Today, when companies set record earnings, it only indicates that they're laying-off American workers, or a nicer, cleaner word would be downsizing. That or having more of their product line made in China at a fraction of what it would cost them to produce the same goods here. Remember a few years ago when the corporate headhunters were buying up companies, cutting the fat, and then selling them? Oh, the term fat refers to the men and women who worked for the company that was being downsized for the purpose of liquidation. Every time it happened, the stock market skyrocketed. It got so I could tell when more people were being pink-slipped just by reading the stock market report in my local newspaper.

When the White House releases a positively glowing gross national product report, they fail to mention that a good majority of the products that make up the GNP are made in China. They're bought by American companies and shipped here, or in the case of companies like Wal-Mart and Mattel, made there by companies who own the factories in China. The goods are then shipped straight to America. Once here, the products are transported to stores throughout this country. Then they are sold to the American consumer. So where does American labor fit into the equation? Aside from the people who handle the products along the way—dock workers, warehouse people, and the like—I'll tell you where: nowhere. China benefits; corporate America benefits, the American manufacturing worker, as always, is left out in the cold. In this situation, he or she does not benefit in any way from the government-reported glowing GNP report, a report that for all practical purposes is a complete fabrication. I'm not against and never have been against companies seeking higher profits. Our capitalistic society is based on strong manufacturing policies, each one created to provide companies the opportunity to increase their profits. But it was also based on competition, the present-day absence of which has continued to play a very significant role in the growing problem that now so seriously affects not only America's middle-class workers, but all Americans, young and old.

OK, so where does this drive for more and more profit end? When does the security and independence of our nation and the welfare of the American people outweigh the importance of the size of a company's bank account? At one time, federal regulations enforced through the U.S. Supreme Court kept corporate powers in balance, or I guess you could say in check. The Supreme Court realized that just as in every facet or mechanism that makes up any society, there comes a time when control over essential industries like oil, companies that supply electricity to communities, food suppliers, and drug manufacturers had to be exercised for the good of society. These controls would never have had to be put in place if true competition were allowed to exist. But today, because of the now apparently legal establishment of monopolies in the above-mentioned industries, corporate-inspired and/or created policies that mask themselves as congressional or senatorial bills have intentionally cleared the way so as to allow corporate entities unrestricted powers. These powers have enabled them to dominate the American marketplace. Our early Supreme Court justices realizing that completely uncontrolled freedoms, whether social or economic in nature, would eventually bring about the type of situation we now face showed exactly were they stood on the issue of monopolies. When in 1892 the Ohio Supreme Court ordered the dissolution of a huge corporation owned by John D. Rockefeller known as Standard Oil. I believe they took this action because they realized the dangers that would eventually follow if monopolies were allowed to exist. The greatest of these we are now seeing manifested in the form of the eventual elimination of America's middle class, the working men and women of America, who make up the backbone of our nation, and who will eventually be forced to join the ever-growing population of working poor. They apparently realized something that our present-day Supreme Court does not care to realize. Too much power in the hands of so few eventually results in abuse of that power and becomes a recipe for social and economic disaster.

As for improving the lives of workers of other nations, that's fine too. We Americans are probably the most generous, giving people on Earth. BUT! I wish the people on Capitol Hill were faithful to a saying that most of us have heard at one time or another. Remember this one? "Charity begins at home." After years of following the track records of these past and present black-hearted politicians as I have, I believe that their one and only policy concerning charity is that it begins and ends everywhere but at home. Their continual actions only reinforce my belief that it is much easier to pilfer the taxpayers' strongbox if billions of dollars are sent over great distances and through as many hands as possible.

Lately, I've been having this recurring dream, one I just can't shake. It's of taxpayers stuffing billions of dollars in a huge bucket. The bucket, being owned by the federal government, is of course full of holes. It's being hurriedly carried from Capitol Hill to Iraq by a president whose face possesses a smile that runs from ear to ear. Moving at breakneck speed, he is being closely pursued by a large horde of extremely overweight, profusely sweating politicians, all pushing and shoving each other while stuffing handfuls of greenbacks in hundreds of what appear to be hastily sewn-on pockets of their suit coats made just for the occasion. Each was wearing a corporate name tag. The only one I could see clearly said Halliburton.

Now, returning to America's generosity and the exportation of American jobs. First of all, the loss of millions upon millions of American jobs has nothing to do with generosity and everything to do with as always, corporate America's bottom line. And our loss is always someone else's gain. In this case the workers of other nations. Of course their lives are better. Why, because now they have our jobs. But just how much better are they? Companies like Wal-Mart and Mattel pay them barely enough to survive, and that's all. This of courser, again results in higher profits for companies while the lives of foreign workers are made just a little less meager. And that, my friend, is what it's all about, just one more step on the road to corporate America's final solution.

An old boss of mine who once owned a heating oil business and has long since departed this world, a gentlemen who I truly believe most likely now resides deep within the depths of the Earth, still in the heating business, once told me never to pay a man one penny more than he's worth. Hmm, seems I recall someone else saying that very same thing. I believe it was a guy named Slade, in the movie, An American Christmas Carol. Oh, and he also said that employees were a dime a dozen. I have to hand it to the man. Right up until his death, he remained true to his opinion. He never saw any difference between a good and a bad employee. We were all the same. I guess that pretty much sums up America's corporate philosophy. Could be that years ago corporate America drafted its own constitution. If they did, the old man I worked for probably was one of its creators and original signers.

CHAPTER THREE

The Motivating Force behind a Global Economy

Through the years, I've read, listened to, and contemplated the whys for allowing foreign investment in America and the reasons prompting the formation of a global economy. One theory rationalizes that if foreign powers have a large-enough financial investment in America they would be much easier to deal with politically, and it would also reduce the possibility of having an armed confrontation with those countries having such large investments.

I believe this line of thought does have some merit, but just how much? If we are dealing with computers programmed to act rationally instead of human beings who more times than not react out of reasons not even remotely connected to the facts that should govern their decisions, the above premise might just work. But to make the possibility of that belief even a little less than probable is the fact that today, just as in the past we've had to deal with human beings. Oh, excuse me, politicians. After all these years I do believe that there is a substantial difference between the two species, one of which usually makes decisions based on whatever logic he or she possesses and the other who makes decisions based on the size of the political contribution or personal financial gain given by whoever. These individuals spend their entire political lives trying to manipulate everyone and every situation, always for personal, financial and/or political gain.

Time and time again, when dealing with what the current administration likes to refer to as rogue nations. Countries like Syria, Iran, and North Korea. We always seem to end up at odds with all involved. Not to mention holding the short end of a very dirty, slippery stick. The same thing holds true for countries like France, China, and Russia. These three nations, besides being well-known political adversaries of the United States, are also big competitors in the world marketplace. Because of this, more times than not. We find one or all three standing between America and its objectives. Their reasons for hindering or blocking our actions, whether they involve imposing NATO sanctions on Iran or, prior to the Iraq war, on Saddam Hussein, are always the same, and always directly or indirectly involve trade agreements that they currently have with those nations. These three very seldom, if ever to be called allies, China, Russia, and France all have financial investments in America. But the fact that they do has never caused a shift in their never-ending support for nations that have stood against us. Even for those who time and time again have openly called for the destruction of the United States.

Are their actions based upon their hatred for America or for the American foreign policies designed by American corporate powers? Or are their decisions strictly profit driven? Or, is it because their political and social philosophies are so completely opposite our own? Whatever their reasons may be, we should all ask ourselves just how advantageous this policy of allowing foreign investment in America's infrastructure has been, and for whom.

Time and time again we have signed trade agreements with China, Mexico, and Japan, just to name a couple, which have called for reductions or in many cases the complete removal of import tariffs, giving these countries what many times amounts to free and complete access to the American marketplace. The removal or reduction of import tariffs as they apply to these countries allows them to market their goods at a substantially lower price than we here in America are able to do. These extremely harmful trade policies have caused these nations to prosper tremendously at the expense of America and the American worker. Rather than reciprocating in kind, these very same nations have continued to keep tariffs high, and in place, on almost if not all U.S. goods that are shipped to their countries. This situation to say the very least has created an un-level playing field for American manufacturers and is also the single most important reason for the tremendous difference in America's swiftly growing and crippling trade deficit. The fact that we cannot compete in today's international marketplace has given unionized and non-unionized corporations still operating in this country a very strong argument when dealing with union contract renewals, allowing them to continually demand wage, benefit, and workforce reductions. While observing these trade agreements for close to forty years, always trying to keep an open mind and allowing both parties the benefit of the doubt. I have continually asked myself who actually benefits from the resulting impact on America. Why would our government—and I use the word "our" very loosely—make trade agreements that were detrimental to America and its people? Who are the real creators of this extremely un-level playing field, and why? Remembering my belief that in government nothing is as it appears and knowing that today the powers in Washington or for that matter in every state in the union are merely representatives of special interest groups and corporate America, the whole trade issue becomes very clear. Their plan is quite simple. More profit can be made if they can force American workers to work at the same or as close to the same wage level as the lowest-wage-paying nation belonging to corporate America's international trade group. Of course, this will mean a more substantial reduction in the quality of life that our nation's working class has enjoyed for so many years. A level and quality of life, that for years has already been purposely chipped away at, and why? Because of corporate America's drive for more and more profit. These extremely large and powerful corporations have eagerly supported if not actually created and drafted the trade agreements that never have or ever will favor the American worker. I sincerely believe that every one of these agreements was written exclusively by law firms representing executives of large national and international corporations. Top ten companies, who for years, have enjoyed a very close working relationship with America's congressional and senate house members, it would also be extremely naive of me to believe that these connection ended at Capitol Hill. When past history, and common sense tells me that they extend all the way to the White House. These negative trade agreements are probably still being drafted by the same individuals for the same reason. The creation of the highest percentage of return possible for the corporate powers that in truth, really run this nation.

In their quest, corporate America has long ago written off compassion, fairness, and loyalty to its nation and its nation's working people. If you believe in the words spoken by President Lincoln during his Gettysburg Address, "A government by the people, for the people," then you must also believe that these government-supported policies are nothing less than treasonous.

As I've said in the preceding pages, our current situation didn't happen over night. For years now, our working men and women have been unable to successfully compete in a game that's been rigged from the very beginning. A game with rules that were created by America's corporate powers, designed to be used continually by them in order to achieve their primary goal of more and more systematic reductions in wages, benefits, and American workforce numbers, all of which would mean a higher level of profit.

Because of the extreme hardship corporate America has placed upon American workers, thousands of people have had to take on a second and even third job. As wages continue to fall, the cost of necessary goods and services has been allowed to rise unjustifiably and unchecked. When the reasons why are questioned, the reply is always the same. Capitalism, according to our political leaders, is the basis for our free society. As such, we have no legal right to restrict any companies attempt to increase their bottom line. Yet in the aftermath of natural disasters such as Katrina, if a retailer doubles or triples the price of plywood, then it's called price gouging. But today, especially under the current administration, it's called capitalism or free enterprise. Please, tell me where the difference lies.

I sincerely believe that for quite a few years now, these increases have all been pre-planned and designed to help further achieve corporate America's "final solution." What we're seeing today is the creation of not only a global economy but also the creation of the largest population of working poor this country has ever seen. This isn't something new. In many parts of the world, people have never known anything but abject poverty and starvation. We usually refer to these places as third-world nations. And why do the people of these nations live the way they do? Simply put, because their countries are being run and controlled by corrupt government officials who are more interested in filling their own offshore bank accounts with the proceeds received from multi-national corporations, than providing decent lives for their people. Sound familiar? In many cases, the governments of these small nations have signed agreements with companies like Exxon Mobil or British Petroleum. Does Union Carbide ring a bell? As we've seen in the past, many of these agreements have given corporations carte blanche, which allowed them to completely ignore health and safety standards. More times than not, the rulers, and in some cases, the relatives of these ruler, become multi-millionaires over night while their people continue to languish in extreme poverty.

In Iraq, a new player in the Iraq-for-sale money game comes in the person of the son of a Texas oil tycoon who just happens to have been a heavy contributor to the election campaign of our current president and the president's father. As of this writing, he or his representatives are negotiating a deal that would allow him to develop oil-rich areas of land controlled by a certain faction in Iraq. Regardless of the fact that this individual or his reps being there violates certain U.S/Iraqi agreements, the Bush administration, in full knowledge of the situation, has completely ignored it.

Contracts worth billions of dollars, not to mention extremely well-paying jobs being awarded to the families of those who contributed heavily to George W. Bush's 2000 and 2004 presidential campaign aren't something new. That's been the Bush administration's policy right from day one. I truly believe that anyone who refuses to believe that favors and favors returned are not the two things that make the wheels of politics go round has to be a person who's in a complete state of denial. After all, that's what politics is all about: In all fairness I have to expand on that by saying that's what life is all about. If we looked at politicians and what they do from a different prospective, if the respected leaders on Capitol Hill were plying their trade on the streets of a big city during the early morning hours. Instead of within the hallowed halls of government, they would be referred to not as senators and congressmen but as whores and hookers. Can you see the comparison? Because of the tremendous amount of financial support given by special interest groups and corporations, a candidates who successfully wins election to the most powerful offices in this land automatically becomes obligated to repay his or her supporters by passing legislation favorable to these financial backers or presenting them with substantial federal contracts, or in the case of the oil tycoon from Texas, the influence necessary to override government policies that have been established between the United States and the Iraqi government.

Let's move on to an extremely important question, one that none of us wants to contemplate or even admit the possibility of ever becoming a reality. But for those of us who for years have watched the direction America is moving, we have to realize that the following possibilities truly do exist.

Will America someday join the list of third-world nations? Can't happen? Think again. Because of the direction America's corporate-controlled government has chosen for us, sometime in the not-too-distant future, America as we know it today will no longer exist, just as America's borders will no longer exist. Small, family-owned businesses will make up a very, very small segment of the American business community. For the most part, companies that today are independently owned will be franchise units owned by national or international conglomerates. Production of all goods will be supplied and strictly controlled on a global scale. For years we've seen this situation in the diamond industry as well as in the marketing of gasoline and heating oil, and let's not forget the pharmaceutical industry. Any future shortages and retail pricing of all goods will be as they have been for years now in those above-mentioned three industries. They will be man-made and designed to create the desired level of demand, which in turn will determine the percentage of profit or return. All this is and will continue to be accomplished by regulating and manipulating the supply. I'm using these industries as examples because at least two are the major players who most effectively determine the economic condition of our society. To many Americans, it's no secret that the OPEC nations have continually been able to create and manipulate the level of demand for oil by closely regulating the amount of crude that they allow on the world market at any one given time. Because such products as gasoline and heating oil, not to mention every commodity that uses oil or a derivative there of in its production or operation, are for all practicable purposes, limitless. The laws governing supply and demand do not apply. The pricing of necessary goods such as gas and heating oil are so crucial to maintaining every American's way of life that just those two products alone can determine how we live and where we will live. The unchecked and uncontrolled pricing of both can and is pushing America's middle class closer and closer to the edge of financial disaster. A growing situation that has already caused the creation of a segment of our society that as I already mentioned closely resembles that of a third-world nation. Those two factors combined with the non-enforcement of our borders and the jailing of border patrol officers who attempt to enforce the laws of our country only reinforces my belief as to the reasons behind the direction America is being pushed in and who's doing the pushing. To answer the question posed by the title of this chapter, only two words come to mind, our old friend's greed and profit.

One morning I turned on one of my favorite TV news programs. The host was commenting on the progress or rather the lack of progress being made by our current administration as it pertains to the war in Iraq. He said that he believed the reason why the president's ratings were so low was because he hadn't changed his policy concerning the handling of the war since day one. When I heard this, I said to myself, "Why change a policy when it's working so well?" The million, no billions of taxpayer dollars are rolling in. Certain privileged companies with close ties to the Oval Office long ago began the job of sewing on as many extra pockets as they could, while opening God only knows how many offshore bank accounts. Only an idiot would fix something that's not broken. Let's face it, looking out from behind the desk in the Oval Office or from a seat in the boardroom of a select number of very influential and politically connected corporations in this country, things look great. No, better than great. Change policy? Not on your life!

CHAPTER FOUR

The Bush Administration,
AKA Corporate America

I realize that I could write an entire book dedicated to the title of this chapter and I also realize it might be considered insignificant and/or irrelevant to America's middle-class economic problem. By those over-the-top supporters of George W. Bush and his administration, although I can't imagine how that conclusion could ever be arrived at.

Never before in the history of this nation has an administration allowed corporate America to operate so completely without federal controls or regulations. Early on, during Bush's first term, it became quite apparent that his administration's method of achieving a successful conclusion for all of its agendas would be by either cutting the funding for agencies whose activities would hamper or obstruct the direction the president and vice president had long ago decided to take America or by instructing certain agencies to disregard or fail to enforce certain laws. The four most important agencies that have become for the most part totally powerless because of these two policies are the Immigration Service, Homeland Security, Border Security, and the Food and Drug Administration. Because of the continued actions or inactions taken by this administration, they not only have diminished the power of these agencies but have knowingly put the health and safety of our nation and its people at risk. I would like to state right now that I have never before seen such a level of unrestricted and unprecedented corporate power, power that has almost overnight led to such monumental price increases in oil, fuel, insurance, and prescription drugs, just to mention a few. I sincerely believe that the current administration and until recently their Republican-controlled Senate and Congress are solely responsible for the tremendous increase in the cost of basic necessities, which in turn has fueled the rapid upswing in the cost of living. An upswing that has, is, and will continue to have devastating effects upon the majority of working-class Americans. With the greatest impact being felt by those located toward the bottom end of the wage scale. They, more than any, now feel the weight of this extremely destructive financial burden. Because of this and the fact that the current administration plays such an important role in corporate America's final solution, I felt I had to write this chapter.

But before we go any farther, I'd like both of us to take a brief look at the two men who lead this nation,

George W. Bush and his second in command, the man who I believe truly wields the real power in the Oval Office, Dick Cheney. Who were these men before they entered the White House, and who were their supporters? Which one had the connections and political clout on Capitol Hill? And of the two, who possesses the intelligence necessary to run the office? Last but not least, what segment of society supplied the millions of dollars in campaign funds that enabled them to amass the largest political war chest in the history of American politics, one that made it possible for them to successfully achieve their 2000 and 2004 presidential victories?

By now, there should no longer be any doubt in anyone's mind as to just who George W. Bush is and who he and his Republican administration represent. For lack of a better description I'd have to say that he and Dick Cheney are the personification of today's corporate America. At this time, I'd like to present a few facts as I understand them, information that the public has at one time or another been subjected to by way of local and national news stories and more cable news programs than I can recount, making this information pretty much public knowledge. After reading the following information, you the reader, can decide for yourself its level of creditability.

There's an old saying that goes something like this: "Judge a man not by what he says, but by what he does," or, "Judge a person not by his words, but by his deeds." Both mean the same, and both are as true today as they were on the day they were first written. So let's take a short look at America's commander in chief and his second in command.

George W. Bush was of eligible age during the 1960s when the war in Viet Nam was going hot and heavy. But he was never drafted and he never served. Why? Because approximately two weeks before his student deferment expired he applied for induction into the Texas Air National Guard. Amazing as it may appear. Mr. Bush was accepted on the very same day he applied. Especially amazing, at least to anyone who was eligible for the draft during that period, is the fact that for most National Guard units throughout the entire country. The waiting list was at least a year and a half long. One more interesting fact is that although he posted the lowest acceptable number of points on the pilot's aptitude test, it apparently wasn't a large enough stumbling block to prevent his being accepted. I was eligible for the draft at the time. Just as all males over the age of eighteen who were considered by the draft board to be able bodied. In those days, it was common knowledge that only the sons of wealthy families who were politically connected or those who had what was referred to as a college deferment had any chance of avoiding the probability of being drafted. It was also common knowledge to those of us who were eligible and lived in New York. The waiting list was closer to three years.

As luck would have it, Mr. Bush somehow ended up number one on the air guard list, and as such, he was immediately sworn in as a member of the Texas Air National Guard. Approximately two weeks after Mr. Bush joined the guard. He was granted a sixty-day leave of absence, which he spent in Florida working on the election campaign of Republican Edward Gurney. Mr. Bush was fortunate enough to be able to take similar leaves of absence during every election season while in the air guard, including one in 1970 so he could work on his father's presidential campaign. In 1972 he once again took a leave of absence in order to work on a campaign in Alabama. I'd like to state right now that for the average guardsman of then and now, leaves of absent were almost nonexistent.

Another one of the many interesting situations that occurred to George W. Bush during his military career came when his company commander approved him for a direct commission to the rank of second lieutenant. This appointment allowed him to avoid the ridiculous, boring, not to mention strenuous process of attending officer's candidate school. A school required for all others except those who exhibited extraordinary skills or who in civilian life held degrees in medicine, law, etc. All those who wished to rise above the ranks of the enlisted men had no choice but to attend OCS; all those that is, except George W. Bush.

Next came flight school where now flight lieutenant George W. Bush began the rigorous training required of all those learning to fly the F-102 Delta Dagger. Can you believe it? Another stroke of good fortune landed right in the lap of our future president when the air force ordered all F-102 units operating overseas, including in Viet Nam, deactivated. As amazing as it seems, this order took effect just three months or approximately twelve weeks after airman Bush graduated from flight school.

I'd like to point out that anyone who has served in the military, as I have, knows that an order such as this becomes common knowledge to all personnel involved well in advance of it ever becoming public. So any thoughts of sending new graduates overseas had been scrapped well before George W. Bush received his wings. During the Viet Nam War many guard units served in the Southeast Asia sector. It appears that Mr. Bush had an angel on his shoulder from day one.

I won't continue delving into all of the recorded events concerning George W. Bush and his time in the air guard. Because it would be a lengthy process and would divert attention away from the main reason this book was written. I'll just mention a couple more items. Approximately halfway through 1972 the military began including the policy of routine drug testing during every serviceman's yearly physical. This time, in order to test for drugs, a urinalysis became part of that exam. Even today, at least as far as I know, the Florida National Guard carries on random drug testing during weekend drills and periods when members are on active duty. From what I understand, members of the Texas Air Guard were routinely questioned about drugs, and examination of nasal cavities in order to check for cocaine use had now become standard operating procedure. For some reason, flight lieutenant Bush never again took another physical, and for some reason, whether connected to the first or not, never attended guard duty again. Of course, for the average soldier an offense such as this would most definitely end in what the army would call an article 15. If the offense occurred repeatedly, a military court marshal could quite possibly be the army's next and last course of action. What was George W. Bush's punishment? He was eventually suspended from fight status. No favoritism there.

Although George W. had what appears to be the easiest enlistment of anyone in the history of any state guard unit, Mr. Bush, for some reason, still couldn't find it within himself to complete the basic enlistment obligation he'd sworn to fulfill. For others, it would have meant the automatic return to 1-A status on the draft list. Instead, he completed the days he missed. I believe only because unlike all the other obstacles he was confronted with, he couldn't find any way of avoiding it. Once he'd accomplished this, he applied for an early release which only under extreme hardship situations have I ever heard of being granted. Although his official discharge from service was dated October 1, 1973. His last actual day was July 31. This meant that his term of service was closer to five years than to the enlistment contract he'd signed designating his term of obligation as being six years.

One last interesting situation arose when Airman Bush asked for and was refused a transfer to a unit in Alabama so he could work there. He solved his dilemma quite easily by not showing up for a year. I served in the active army during the same time Mr. Bush was enlisted with the air guard. Actually, I was released from active duty at the end of 1970. At the time, if a soldier was absent from duty, he was considered absent without leave or AWOL. I believe that after thirty days the charge was always upgraded to desertion. What punishment was levied against Mr. Bush? : N O T H I N G, ZERO: I'm not sure if you the reader realize this. But after George W's less than stunning military record became public and was reported by a leading news journalist. A man, who till this day I and I'm sure millions of Americans still have all the respect in the world for, was fired. Why, because he foolishly reported it. After that, no one, but no one in the media would touch the story. After I did a little research on the Internet, I found out who actually brought the Bush military service record to the public's attention. To the best of my knowledge the story came from a very prestigious paper located in the Boston area. Because I was interested in getting my hands on the original story, I sent an e-mail to them asking for a copy. To this day, I have never received a reply from that e-mail. Why? Why did the Boston paper and the entire American news media drop the Bush story like a hot rock? Is it possible that the Bush administration. An administration known in the past to have sought out revenge from individuals who spoke publicly against Bush Policy had used its tremendous power in order to halt all investigations into the president's time in the air guard? Will we ever know the truth? I sincerely doubt it. We'll just have to write it off as another unsolved mystery. I guess it's up to each one of us to decide on the level of Mr. Bush's patriotism, courage, and devotion to his country, and also the credibility of the above information.

Now, let's take a look at Dick Cheney and his reaction to our nation's call to duty. Although Mr. Cheney, like George W. Bush, was of military age at the time of the Viet Nam War, he was able to successfully avoid service to his country by obtaining five separate college deferments. During an interview in 1989 Mr. Cheney told a reporter that "he had other priorities." Well Mr.

Cheney, I, like thousands of other guys who were eligible for the draft, also had, as you described it, other priorities. But the federal government didn't recognize ours. So we went, and we served; we served, even though many of us disagreed with the war myself included. We served, even though it would have been much easier to have sought college deferments or made a mad dash for Canada and safety as thousands of others did. But many of us chose to serve because we felt as Americans we had an obligation to defend our nation's policies. For thousands of young Americans, that decision cost them their lives. Years later, the knowledge that I have today about the reasons behind our involvement in Viet Nam and the pardons that were later given to those who ran. Has made me and I imagine many others feel betrayed. Oh, and the reason we sacrificed those thousands upon thousands of American lives in a war we could never win or maybe never intended to win. A war extremely similar to the one in Iraq--- was it politics? Was it in order to fill the bank accounts of certain corporations like Hughes Aircraft? The millions of taxpayer dollars that funded that war, some of which I understand came from our Social Security System, are long gone now. And with it, thousands of American lives. And the reasons why? Aside from Viet Nam being a money-making project. Anyone who tells you it was for freedom or to stop communism in its tracts has accepted the false rhetoric that continually came out of the White House during the 1960s and early seventies. Rather than accept the truth. That truth being, that every life that was lost in Viet Nam, achieved nothing. Today, Viet Nam's government is communist. That being the case how can we justify the war? How can we justify the millions of American, Cambodian and Vietnamese lives lost? We can't. We lost, the Vietnamese people lost. Everyone lost except the merchants of death who supplied the means that enabled that war to become a grim, horrific reality. It's just politics.

To say I didn't enjoy my time in the military would be an understatement. But to this day, except for the slight still remaining feeling of having been betrayed. I never regretted those three years of service. And as a sole surviving son, I could have used a provision in the draft regulations in order to skirt what at the time I truly believed to be every American's obligation. But if I had, for the rest of my life I would have had to carry a feeling of guilt that I'd created by not serving and the shame of knowing that someone might have died in my place. I wonder how many of our nation's leaders have ever felt the joy of being alive, while at the same time, felt a strange sort of guilt, because they still were? No, didn't think so.

OK! Now that we know how our nation's two leaders handled their obligations to their country. Let's move on and briefly discuss their business and political careers.

George W. Bush Jr. made a great deal of money from his involvement in three businesses—Arbusto Energy, Inc., Spectrum 7, and Harken Energy Corp. In each one of his financial undertakings, his contributions are somewhat hard to perceive. But the overall pattern he established during his business career is extremely important because it's also a good indication of the level of business savvy and competence he did or did not possess. How did G.W. achieve such a high level of financial success when From all accounts, it seems that Bush Jr. did very little actual work during his time in the business world. A cynical person might even say that all three of the positions Mr. Bush held were equivalent to what might be referred to as no-show jobs secured solely because of his family's political and financial connections.

Using $20,000 of his own money, George Jr., just as his father before him, jumped headlong into the oil business by establishing a company that he named Arbusto which in English translation means Bush. The fifty or so investors in George Jr's new company were for the most part friends of his uncle's. All together they had invested approximately $4.7 million but eventually ended up walking away with empty pockets. A friend of the Bush family told a local paper that all who invested in Arbusto ended up on the short end, cashing out with somewhere in the neighborhood of twenty cents on the dollar.

Just weeks, maybe even days, before Arbusto reached the brink of bankruptcy, Spectrum 7 Energy Corporation purchased it. If my memory serves me correctly, I believe it was in September of 1984. Even though George W.'s performance was quite a bit less than lackluster while operating his first business venture, the new owners saw fit to install him as the president of Spectrum, while at the same time giving him 13.6 percent of the parent company's stock. Although Spectrum 7 was a small oil company, it was owned by two very wealthy Texas residents. As all of us living in the real world know, with wealth, comes, power. The more wealth, the more power, and these two guys weren't only wealthy. They were a couple of real powerhouses who were also very well politically connected Republicans. That's where the power comes in. Together, both were also involved in another little business. They were the owners of the Texas Rangers baseball team. Because these two wealthy philanthropists were also a couple of down-to-earth, good ole boys, not to mention extremely generous, and knowing how much George liked baseball, they gave Bush Jr. the opportunity to purchase a piece of the team at what can only be described as a bargain-basement price. Some time later, George Jr. sold that piece for at least twenty times more than he paid for it.

A short few months after purchasing Arbusto and installing Bush Jr. as president, Spectrum 7 suffered losses amounting to somewhere in the neighborhood of $400,000. The size of the loss proved to be too great for the company to absorb or want to absorb, and soon Spectrum took a direction that was quite familiar to its new president. Just as before, and I might add once again, just in the nick of time, another company by the name of Harken Energy came to the rescue when it bought Spectrum 7 lock, stock, and barrel. Isn't it amazing how by living a good and righteous Christian life everything always seems to work out? Another thought just entered my mind. Is it possible that Spectrum 7 was just a vehicle used to move George W. up the ladder and at the same time provide him with a favorable, at least if one doesn't look to closely, business resume? Business credentials that later on would come in handy when he entered politics? That was just a thought. G.W.'s problems, if he had any, ended when Harken purchased Spectrum 7. Actually, they didn't just end. You see, Life for George W. only got better and better, especially after he walked away with $227,000 worth of Harken stock and a position on Harken's board of directors. Oh, and the salary? How does $80,000 to $100,000 a year strike you? His position on Harken's board of directors lasted well into the 1990s. While there, he was allowed to purchase Harken stock at somewhere near 40 percent below face value and was also allowed to borrow $180,000 from Harken at an extremely low rate of interest. Did Bush Jr. ever repay that loan? Considering that Harken forgave $340,000 in loans to several executives, of whom I believe G.W. was probably one, I sincerely doubt it.

Considering the size of the salary Bush Jr. was being paid, the board of directors must have considered him to be a tremendous asset. But what did he actually do? What made him so valuable? That's pretty hard to say, but things, very good things, began happening for Harken after G.W. joined its board of directors. First, it received a $25 million stock offering from a very unusual source: a bank that had known CIA connections. Harken also received a drilling contract with a small Middle East country called Bahrain. The drilling contract occurring around the same time as an Arab member of Harken's board of directors was invited to sit in on White House policy meetings with George W.'s father, President George Bush Sr., and National Security Adviser Brent Scowcroft. The firm's 25 million in stock offerings was guaranteed by an Arkansas bank named Stephens Inc. whose CEO, Jackson Stephens, was also a member of President Bush's Team 100, an exclusive group of individuals, each whom had given at least $100,000 to his presidential campaign committee. Instead of placing the offering directly with Harken, Stephens placed it with the London subsidiary of Union Bank of Switzerland, a bank that had never been known to be an investor in small American companies.

In June of 1990 George Jr. pulled off another stroke of genius when he sold 60 percent of his Harken stock for $848,560. Once again, his good fortune, sharp business savvy or maybe the guardian angle that sat upon his shoulder caused him to make what on the outside appeared to be a very shrewd business move. Why? Because in August, Iraq invaded Kuwait and Harken stock dropped 25 percent. Not long after, a large quarterly loss caused its stock to fall even farther. In May, approximately one month prior to G.W. unloading his stock in Harken, the White House received a State Department memo warning that Saddam Hussein had gone over the edge and was no longer controllable. The memo also listed several options for responding to him, including an oil ban that could quite possibly have an impact on U.S. oil prices. Being an individual with a very inquisitive nature, my question is this. Bush Jr., whose father was president at the time and because of the national security issues involved, had no doubt been briefed or at least read that memo. This being the case, it makes me wonder if the president ever discussed the situation in Iraq with his son. Being a father myself, and if faced with a similar situation and knowing a word or two could save my son or daughter thousands of dollars, I think I'd find it extremely hard not to do so. But on the other hand, I suppose one could ask a nationally known famous home-decorating expert and celebrity what happens when someone outside the Washington loop receives what on Wall Street is commonly referred to as "insider trader information." Could it be that her legal problems might never have come about if her dad were a sitting president? I'm just giving you, the reader a little food for thought.

I could continue on with even more factual information pertaining to Bush's business career, but I believe that at this point it is extremely easy to see just how G.W. was able to acquire the personal wealth he now enjoys. It also appears to me that the level of success achieved by George W. Bush was not so much the results of his knowledge of business or his intelligence or his leading the good and righteous life that I'm sure he lives. But rather his riding the wave of success that was created by the business, political, and personal relationships his father had created over the years. That, plus his access to the power and influence his father wielded as president of the United States at the time.

Now, let's take a brief look at our nation's vice president, Mr. Richard Cheney. As far as I'm able to conclude, Mr. Cheney had two or three close calls with the draft. But with a smart move here and there—college deferments, getting married, and a quick stint in graduate school—he was able to successfully avoid serving his country. In January of 1967 Cheney turned twenty-six and was no longer eligible for military service.

In 1969, two years after beating the draft, Mr. Cheney began his political career. In that year he became an intern in the Nixon administration. Some time after Mr. Cheney began his internship, he secured a job in the office of Donald Rumsfeld, who from 1969 to 1970 held the position of director of the Office of Economic Opportunity. In the years that followed Mr. Cheney held a number of positions: White House staff assistant in 1971, assistant director of the Cost of Living Council from 1971 to 1973, and deputy assistant to the president from 1974 to 1975. From 1973 to 1974 Mr. Cheney left public service, accepting a position in the private sector as vice president of the investment firm of Bradley, Woods, and Company.

After his two-year stint as vice president of Bradley, Woods, and Company, Mr. Cheney accepted a new position as assistant to then-president Ford. At that time, Donald Rumsfeld, who oversaw Ford's White House transition team, moved up the ladder to become Ford's chief of staff. Shortly afterward, Mr. Rumsfeld was named secretary of defense and Dick Cheney moved up the political ladder when he replaced Rumsfeld as chief of staff. Together, Cheney and Rumsfeld were able to have William Colby removed from his position as director of the Central Intelligence Agency so they could replace him with one of their own political allies, George Hiram Walker Bush. His installation as head of the CIA created what would become a long-lasting political alliance between the future president, Richard Cheney, and Donald Rumsfeld, one that still lasts to this day.

In 1976, Dick Cheney became campaign manager for Gerald Ford's presidential bid. It was at this time that he found himself working alongside Gerald Ford's campaign chairman, Mr. James Baker, a man who was no stranger to Capitol Hill and one who through numerous Washington connections had more than a considerable amount of political clout. In 1978 Mr. Cheney ran and won election to the U.S. House of Representatives, representing Wyoming. He was re-elected to office five times.

I have one more small bit of information that I believe just might give us a little insight into the political ideology of Mr. Cheney, as well as George W. Bush and the Bush administration, insight that may allow us to understand the reasoning behind the Bush administration's unbendable foreign policy as it refers to America's current war in Iraq and the president's continuing hard line when dealing with Iran. In 1997 William Kristol and Robert Keegan, both well-known in Washington political circles, founded what was described as an American neoconservative think tank called "Project for the New American Century." From what I've read, the supporters and quite possibly a good majority of their membership can be found at the highest levels of the Bush administration. Could it be possible that Vice President Cheney and President Bush are among the membership? Because the goal most central to the creation of this organization, to promote worldwide American leadership through military strength, diplomatic energy, and commitment to moral principles, appears to mirror the Bush- Cheney policy concerning Afghanistan, Iraq, and Iran. I myself cannot discount the possibility that if in fact they are members. One thing all of us found out later on is undeniably clear: Truth was apparently not included in the organization's by-laws

Dick Cheney's numerous political appointments and the offices he held go on and on, also to include Republican minority whip and secretary of state. But instead of continuing, let's just say that because of his years of successful public service and the people he'd come to know, there's no doubt that Dick Cheney was and is what in Washington political circles is referred to as a heavy hitter.

Let's move on to the job that probably gave him the largest return of any investment he'd ever made, that being the CEO of Halliburton. In 1995 Mr. Cheney served as chairman of the board and chief executive officer of Halliburton, a fortune 500 Company that was and still is involved in a multitude of enterprises, some of which involve contracts with the federal government. While still serving as CEO of Halliburton, Mr. Cheney accepted the task of heading up George W. Bush's vice-presidential search committee. After carefully looking over Mr. Cheney's recommendations, George Bush Jr. surprised his political colleagues by asking Dick Cheney himself to join the Republican ticket. (Let's run that last bit of pre-2000 presidential election history through our thought processes once or twice.) I find it extremely hard to believe it was a surprise, at least to those who occupied George W. Bush's inner circle. I do, however, believe it to be the kind of statement we the forgotten people have gotten used to hearing from the Bush administration. I personally believe that Mr. Cheney was selected by the financial backers of George W. Bush's presidential campaign and no one else.

Politicians are created in much the same way as General Mills markets a box of their cornflakes, and for years now, they've also contained just about as much substance. The Republican Party, AKA corporate America, knew that if they were going to win the upcoming presidential election. They needed a candidate who would appeal to the voters. It really didn't matter whether or not he was the kind of a guy who was ahead of the curve on social, economic, and world problems. It also didn't really matter whether or not he was a bit less than a genius. No, the man they needed had to appear clean cut and outdoorsy, the kind of guy who lives next door or someone you might see at your local supermarket, and since the Republican Party was courting the Christian coalition in order to grab their vote, their candidate had to be perceived as a down-to-earth, devoted Christian, the type you and I could relate to, or maybe look at and see a JFK or a Bill Clinton. Someone the majority of American voters could identify with.

But who would be the real force behind corporate America's choice for president? That's where Dick Cheney came in. One quick look at both resumes tells the story. Who had all the connections on Capitol Hill? Who had a successful history in politics and business? Who knew where the bodies were buried? Knew the secrets that could be used to pressure the right people and push the right buttons? The guy who could get passed the legislation that big business wanted? Was it George W. Bush, I hardly thing so. Even with his father's connections. I doubt that he could be anywhere near as effective as Dick Cheney. So, who's the real power in the Oval Office? Who pulls the strings that make George W. dance? I believe that corporate America is the real power. Dick Cheney is their messenger.

Because of the major role the presidential victory of George W. Bush and Dick Cheney played in connection with advancing corporate America's final solution, I felt it imperative that I put into chronological order as best I can what I've read and believe to be true. What follows are the sequence of events that allowed corporate America's direct and most powerful representatives to successfully scale the walls of 1600 Pennsylvania Ave. and the present and future effects his administration's policies have had and will continue to have on America and America's middle class. After George W. Bush's first win, the American people rejoiced at the prospect of a new and better tomorrow, a tomorrow that we all found out very early on would never come.

I'd now like to mention one thing that has always amazed me. It's the fact that so many Americans have no idea what the Republican or Democratic Party stand for. In the case of the Democrats I can understand and forgive that. Because how can any of us know when they don't know themselves? Or do they? Years ago, back in the good ole days, they represented the working class. But as the years passed, big money began oozing through the cracks in the walls of integrity that surrounded and protected their basic political and social philosophies. Today, the differences seen between the parties when dealing with our nation's major issues have become less and less obvious, almost to the point of being indistinguishable. One fact, however, common to both present-day parties is undisputable; the fact being that whatever legislation one or both parties support is just about always detrimental to the American voting majority.

When it comes to defining the Republican Party it's always been very easy because they've always represented big business. They've always represented the upper 10 percent in this country and they never completely denied it. How could they?

They've always advocated lower taxes for the rich based on at least their publicly expressed belief that millions of extra dollars in the pockets of the rich would automatically mean more investment in America, translating into more jobs. Through the years they've repeatedly proclaimed and pushed this philosophy even while knowing that foreign investments have become much more lucrative than investments at home, and that fact alone would undoubtedly direct the flow of American investments and consume the greatest portion of those millions of dollars the rich were able to keep because of Republican-backed tax cuts.

They also continue espousing their claim of record growth and great jobs, which I suppose could be accepted as being true for the average blue-collar worker who has lived most of his or her life within the walls of a monastery. But ask the men and women on the streets of America. Ask the people who drag themselves out of bed each and every morning, the majority of whom are up before daylight so they can be on time for the first of the two or in some cases even three jobs that many now need just to keep their heads above water. Once you've talked to a few of these people, I believe the Republican great economy fairytale will end abruptly.

Is the Bush administration telling the American people the truth? If they are, it would be the first time since G.W. took the oath of office, an oath pledging to defend our Constitution, an oath I believe he never intended to honor. I've always firmly believed that a person or people of considerable persuasion could continue telling a dying man how great he looks, and if they repeated it enough times, the poor guy would believe them. He'd believe them right up to the end. Let's be honest about it and give credit where credit is due. The Bush administration has provided hundreds, no, millions of new jobs. Of course, knowing how great those jobs are is just about impossible for us to discover unless we read about them in the world news section of one of our local papers. Why? Because the vast majority of these new jobs are located in places like China and Japan and let's not forget a few third-world countries. I guess obtaining one of those great jobs would make the morning commute a little less than desirable.

Let's use China as an example. Employees working for a company that makes articles for Wal-Mart live in dormitories and are charged for the privilege of doing so. Oh, they don't have to live there. They can live somewhere else. But they still have to pay for the living area they no longer use. Oh, wages? How does three dollars a day strike you? Keep that number in mind. Why, because sometime in the future, you as an American worker may be working for a wage that resembles it. One last reason why the probability of an American landing one of these great three-dollar-a-day jobs is extremely slim is the fact that the countries where these new jobs are so plentiful probably have immigration laws that would prohibit the average undocumented immigrant, Americans included, from working within their borders without the government's permission. Oh God, how old fashioned and out of date, right George?

The fact is that over the last twenty or thirty years this country has lost millions upon millions of decent-paying jobs, all which have been replaced, if replaced at all, with rock-bottom, low-paying jobs. As hard as it is for some of us to believe or accept, there are working men and women in this country who will spend tonight, tomorrow night, and quite possibly the rest of their lives showering at work while living in tents or cardboard packing crates. I know, you're now probably thinking to yourself this guy's crazy. Stuff like that doesn't happen here in America, the land of plenty, or these people would probably be living like that anyway. Oh, I'm sure you're right about a certain percentage of these people. But I also believe that if America's employment and wage situation was not as it is today, that percentage would be very small.

You see, people without hope, people who have seen their way of life slip away—no, not slip away; I think taken or ripped away would best describe it—have been forced to struggle harder and harder in order to just keep a roof over their family's heads and food on the table, many only to eventually lose their battle and end up being forced to join the ranks of families who have already fallen victim to the insatiable profit-at-any-cost policies of corporate America. Lower wages when combined with what for all appearances looks like government-supported price gouging, passed off as simply the rising cost of living or just the natural scheme of things common to our capitalistic society. One by one, American families find themselves drowning in what I can only describe as a rapidly growing sea of despair. In America, this group or segment of our society is still a minority. But their numbers are growing rapidly, courtesy of our, excuse me their senators, congressmen, and corporate America's final solution. A close friend I once knew who has long since passed on had a saying that never fit so well when discussing modern-day politics and politicians: "Figures lie and liars figure." The national statistics concerning the rate of unemployment are a perfect example of the true meaning of that saying. Once someone has used up their total allotted number of weekly unemployment benefits, their name is removed from the monthly and then quarterly unemployment statistics. They are still unemployed, but now they're also invisible to a government that runs on statistics, facts, and figures that they manipulate daily in order to support their claims and their policies. Mark Twain once wrote, "The difference between government and people is that people care." His words were right then and still are today.

As I stated at the beginning of my book, nothing in politics is ever as it appears. I'd now like to add to that by saying, "Or as it's told to the American people." Over the years and on several occasions I've heard people say that whenever the government tells you anything, the first thing you have to realize is that they're lying to you. Sadly, I and many others believe the reasons behind our entering the war in Iraq were predicated on lies designed to cover up what was and always will be strictly a financial undertaking, a financial expedition that had and still has nothing at all do with weapons of mass destruction. WMD's that UN inspectors, along with American intelligence, repeatedly told the Bush administration Saddam no longer possessed, weapons he at one time did have only because they were given or sold to him by prior U.S. administrations, one in particular headed by George W. Bush's father. The sale of which probably came about because of the influence of lobbyists representing American and/or international weapons manufacturers. Every government, every ruler since the creation of the first weapon and men who were willing to use them, all had to have a reason justifying their use. It was at that time the term war became part of man's vocabulary, and it was also around the same time that we were first introduced to the arms' merchants, the dealers in death and destruction. Yes, even back in the days prior to the Crusades men were making money selling weapons. Descendents of those first arms' merchants still ply their trade today. On Capitol Hill, besides being called company reps., they're referred to as lobbyists.

"Remember the Maine!" That phrase was extremely useful when American interests wanted to go to war against Spain who at the time occupied Cuba. As every student of history knows, every war ever waged had to have a slogan or slogans that would stir the hearts of the people, especially the young. Slogans that would instill within the youth of their nation the emotion and desire that would make them eager to fight and die for whatever cause, real or fabricated, necessary or unnecessary, in whatever war the corporate powers of that nation decide to become involved. As we all know, it's much easier to motivate people to kill one another if they're pissed off at each other. As in the case of the Spanish American war, many years after it ended historians, after exhaustive investigation, concluded that the explosion on the

battleship Maine. The incident that provided the necessary spark that caused America to invade Cuba was most
likely caused not by a hostile act, but by the Maine's mal-
functioning boiler. But, that's all water over the bridge,
dam, or whatever. And the Americans who died in the
hills and valleys of Cuba? Hell, they were going to die
sooner or later anyway. These days, governments AKA
corporate powers have a much nicer way of classifying or
maybe a better word would be desensitizing the horrors
of war. They lump all the civilian casualties together and
call them collateral damage. The average man or woman
on the street would never associate these two words with
their actual meaning, which in realistic terms means the
maiming, death, and destruction of hundreds, even thousands of innocent men, women, and children, human beings. It means hundreds of body parts strewn everywhere
after a suicide attack or battle. It means the God-awful
stench of rotting bodies and seeing rats, sometimes even
dogs. All fighting each other for the chance of grabbing
a quick meal compliments of the dead bodies. It means
scenes I refuse to imagine or describe. So in order to make
such things more palatable to the people back home, the
phrase collateral damage is used. Hey! It's a squeaky-clean
term that doesn't come near to describing what it really
means. It's a word people can hear without being upset.
It's a word they can hear and still continue eating their
dinner.

The assassination of Archduke Franz Ferdinand and
his wife was just one more excellent reason or the excuse
needed to start WWI. After all, the death of two individuals is as good a reason as any to kill millions. Hell,

in upstate New York where I grew up, we lost more than two people every first snowfall.

Why Vietnam? The politically correct explanation is that then-president Eisenhower wanted to stop communism from spreading past the seventeenth parallel. But honestly, to this day, I'm willing to bet that there are thousands of Americans who served the country at the time who if being honest with themselves. Still don't know the real reason. But you can bet your boots that money played a large part in it.

Now, along comes the Bush administration. While they were talking overtime about sanctions and peace, George W. Bush and Vice President Dick Cheney were hastily picking through intelligence reports until they found or created the information they had to have in order to justify the war on Iraq. As we all discovered later on, these facts were not just inaccurate. They were downright lies fed to Congress, the Senate, and the American people. All used to accomplish the Bush administration's desired results.

Going back in time to at least six months, and let's face it quite possibly even prior to his presidential victory of 2000, even before any talk of war was publicly discussed. Halliburton, the company that Vice President Cheney once headed up, a company that on more than one occasion had already faced allegations of overcharging or plainly put defrauding the government and the American taxpayers. Representatives of this pillar of business met with high-ranking government officials, and by the end of their meeting or meetings, they were given an exclusive, $7 billion dollar, no-bid contract to provide services for a war that the Bush administration denied it was planning. To make matters appear worse, statements have been made indicating that the no-bid contract process, the first of many awarded to Halliburton, was arranged and coordinated through Vice President Cheney's office; surprise, surprise. This was going on at the very same time or even prior to asking the all important question of whether or not Iraq still possessed weapons of mass destruction. An issue that was still in the investigation stages at the UN and during the same period that UN inspectors had stated repeatedly that Saddam no longer had such weapons. Don't get me wrong. I'm not saying Saddam wasn't a threat. Even without WMDs. If he wasn't a threat at the time, sometime in the future he definitely would be. But for the Bush administration to initiate a war based on lies was, is, and always will be wrong. Only after every alternative has been exhausted and you find you have no other choice, then, and only then, can war become the only option left. When that option is exercised, you go to win or you stay at home. In Iraq, G.W. and Richard Cheney did not go to win. They went to war in order to redistribute our nation's wealth. That's right, from the vaults of the U.S. Treasury to the bank accounts of companies like Halliburton.

I feel I have to discuss the war not only because it plays such a substantial role in advancing corporate America's agenda. But it also shows, at least to me, just how indifferent the Bush administration and America's corporate powers are when it comes to weighing the lives of human beings against the bottom line. It also shows just how far they were willing to go in order to get their hands on the pot of gold that lay at the end of the rainbow. The pot of gold I'm referring to was the largest treasury balance this nation has ever seen. And the rainbow, that began wherever George W. Bush kicked off his campaign, and ended with the Supreme Court's verification of his 2000 presidential victory. As I see it, the war in Iraq was planned well in advance, and only George W. Bush, Dick Cheney, and high-level Halliburton executives will ever know just how far. A war such as the one in Iraq was the only event large enough to provide the publicly acceptable excuse that would allow the Bush-Cheney-Halliburton administration to gut the U.S. Treasury without major resistance from Congress, the Senate, and the American people. Only something the size of a costly war could have justified the billions upon billions of taxpayer dollars that were going to be spent, or maybe the right word would be stolen.

I'd like to go on record right now as saying that I support the troops 100 percent. I'm an army vet who served in the 1960s so I know a little something about an unpopular war.

I feel a very deep sorrow for all the men and women who have been maimed and killed in Afghanistan and Iraq. I guess that here is where some of my readers and I may part company. You see, I place the entire blame for their injuries and deaths and the deaths of hundreds of thousands of innocent Iraqi and Afghanistan people squarely on the shoulders of George W. Bush, Dick Cheney, and all the corporations they represent, including Halliburton.

Over the years I've watched as negative legislation has been pushed through Capitol Hill, and I've also watched the changes in America caused by the passage of such legislation. It is because of my years of observing the corrupt political process in America that I've come to the conclusion that I mentioned at the beginning of this book, that conclusion being that accidents in politics are far and few between. Even when for all appearances something that occurs looks quite accidental and is perceived by the public as just a simple slip of the tongue. The reason behind it could very likely be just the opposite. As I've already stated, the chances of anything coming out of Washington being a mistake is extremely remote. I believe this because even though a good majority of Americans wrongly perceive today's politicians as not having the brains God gave a rock, they are in reality as sly as the slyest fox and as slick as the snake that inhabited the tree in the Garden of Eden. All actions carried out by these individuals are highly calculated long before they're ever arrived at. In order to aid these multi-faced individuals, whose principles change as regularly as you and I change our socks, millions of dollars are spent every year not just by political parties but also by the administrations that are in power or hope to be in power after the next election. Every one of these dollars is used to fund what are called "think tanks." People employed by these think tanks exhaustively research and study, among other things, the reactions of the voting public when subjected to thousands of different scenarios. Every presidential speech, every word spoken at any Capitol Hill press conference is always read from a carefully orchestrated script, and anyone representing the administration who upon reading any official statement, repeatedly deviates too far from the actual script could quite possibly find him or herself standing at the end of an unemployment line. And anyone who's been there knows what that means. If employment prospects fail to improve for those individuals, and fast, they just might find themselves joining the ranks of the invisible.

Corporate America uses think-tank techniques when marketing their products. It appears to me that the very same marketing procedure used to sell a box of cornflakes is also used, and I might add, very successfully, when trying to sell a presidential candidate, which, realistically is just another product. In both cases, whether we're talking about the design and color arrangement used on the box of cornflakes or the outward appearance of the candidate, plus the sixty or more seconds of commercial crap that accompanies both, it amounts to the same basic marketing technique that sells or does not sell both products. This technique, at least when referring to consumer goods is usually successfully limited to the first time a product or service is purchased. After that, how efficiently the product works determines whether or not the consumer will buy it again. But in the case of the Bush administration and politics in general, this rule does not apply.

Over the years, and not just in the stores, every one of us has been sold some pretty nasty stuff, the difference being that when we find that a product stinks, we immediately toss it in the trash. But when it comes to the politicians we elect, we have to keep eating the crap they feed us for four years before we can throw them out, and believe you me, we're all pretty damn sick of doing so by the time the next election rolls around.

I'd like to take a moment to say something about the congressional hearings on oil and other government and/or corporate wrongdoings, hearings that most of us have watched on TV, read of, or heard about. After observing a few of these comedy specials, it is apparent, at least to me, that the people we elect to run our nation and protect our way of life all appear to have Alzheimer's disease. That or they're the biggest damn liars under the sun. I'll let you decide that for yourselves. An excellent example showing just how great the level of senility in government is occurred when the identity of one of our government CIA agents was accidentally, and I sincerely doubt it, leaked to the news media by someone very close to the Oval Office, someone whose name no one could remember.

Now, returning to the war in Iraq for a moment, I'd like to more fully explain why I believe this ill-conceived mismanaged war was and is in reality very well managed. It was never the Bush administration's intention to win in Iraq. Oh, if a win did result, that would of course be a plus. But the real goal behind the war was for the most part financial. Maybe the possibility of the events that followed was never fully anticipated by George W. Bush and his pal Dick Cheney. But let's face it. A high school freshman with a little knowledge of Middle East history or any individual with the mental capacity that would allow them to remember what happened to the Russians in Afghanistan could have most likely predicted our current situation in Iraq. Why not the Bush administration? For me to explain the reasons for my position concerning the quagmire we call Iraq and the time line when corporate America really began its campaign aimed at capturing the White House, or more accurately, the United States Treasury and the American people. I'd like you the reader to join me in taking one giant step backward. Count to ten and clear your mind of as many prejudices as you are capable of. Take a deep breath. Now, let's take a look back in time. How about a few months? How about four years? No, I think in order to get a more accurate picture of what transpired in 2000 we'd have to go back at least eight-plus years prior to the first Bush administration.

The Republicans were out and the Democrats were in. It goes without saying that corporate America's front organization, the Republican Party, wanted back in. But with the Clinton administration's record, which eventually included the highest positive balance in the history of our treasury, they knew it wasn't going to be easy. They also realized that in order for their plan to succeed it had to be damn close to perfect. The chances of being defeated had to be reduced to the smallest percentile.

Because I'm like you and not privileged to see the information only insiders of political parties are, I can only base my beliefs and writings on my conclusions gleaned from what I've read, and here they are. Sometime following the 1980 presidential election Jeb Bush and his family moved to Florida. In 1986, he became heavily involved in Dade county politics, helping in the election campaign of Mr. Bob Martinez, who won that election and became governor of Florida. In return for Jeb Bush's support, Governor Martinez appointed him as Florida's secretary of commerce. At the time I read this, two questions puzzled me about Jeb's move to the Sunshine State. Question number one: Having so many other states to choose from, why Florida? Number two: Why did he leave Texas in the first place? After a little research, both my questions were answered. The answer to the first automatically answered the second. Anyone who has followed Florida's political history especially in connection with past presidential elections realizes that Florida has always been what politicians refer to as a pivotal state. This means that the electoral votes from the state of Florida can in the future as they have in the past decide the winner of a close presidential election. Could this be why Jeb Bush made the move? Is it even remotely possible that he was sent to Florida by his father and/or the hierarchy of the Republican Party, and if so, why?

Jeb served from 1987 to 1988. Pretty short run! He resigned so he could work on his dad's presidential campaign. Get the picture? Ole Jeb, undoubtedly under the tutelage of his father, was racking up political favors and points all along the way, things he needed if he were to succeed in his still-unknown-to-the-public quest for something much larger. A couple of years later, 1994 to be exact, Jeb, along with the backing the of the Republican party, went after what for most of us thought was that larger something when he launched an unsuccessful campaign bid against Florida incumbent Lawton Chiles. George Hiram Walker Bush, the Republican Party, and corporate America not being the kind of people who throw in the towel, once again backed Jeb in his 1998 second attempt at winning the Florida governorship. This time, running against Democratic hopeful Mr. Buddy

MacKay, the outcome was a completely different story: Jeb won. His second time around proved to be a charm. I'm not going to say that because his brother George was the governor of Texas and his dad a recent president of the United States who had millions of dollars within his reach and access to the most influential republican politicians in America had helped Jeb in his quest. But in my mind, it sure as hell didn't hurt. I do, however, believe that because of Lawton Chile's overwhelming support in the state of Florida, a second run against Chiles would have resulted in another defeat for Jeb Bush.

Thanks to the Republican machine that backed him for a second time. Jeb was now Florida's forty-third governor. Having been a resident and registered voter during his two terms in office, I can't honestly say anything that would detract from his service to the people of Florida other than his slightly less than apparent connection to the 2000 election and maybe his policies concerning Florida schools. Putting those issues aside, I believe that Jeb has much more feeling and compassion for the American people than does his brother George. Because of this, I also believe he lacks the qualifications corporate America demands of a presidential candidate. I may be wrong in my assessment, but I believe that Governor Bush has a little too much humanity to qualify him as a presidential candidate, at least in the eyes of the power brokers who control the White House. I also believe, and naturally so, that Jeb gained not just politically but also financially from his association with the Republican Party and its corporate backers. Over the years I've observed the rise of a few junior politicians and it has become apparent that if a fledgling up-and-comer, especially the son of a former president and ex-head of the Central Intelligence Agency, did as he was told, it was only natural that big bucks and lucrative political positions would automatically come his way

If I were asked to sum up Governor Bush's time in office, I would have to say that on the majority of the issues that faced him, he was pretty much a middle-of-the-road governor, and personally I believe the best thing he did while in office was to successfully defeat, at least for the time being, the mass transit bill that would have crippled Florida's taxpayers for decades to come.

Until George W. Bush began his 2000 campaign for the White House I, like I believe most people, thought that Jeb's quest to become governor of Florida was his only goal. Like most voters, I never saw the connection or the true reasoning behind Jeb Bush's run for the office of governor. Once the 2000 presidential election was over, it should have become apparent to all who follow politics that Jeb's win was just one more piece in a plan designed to further guarantee his brother's successful run for the presidency, a plan that had been years in the making, a plan that near the end of the 2000 presidential campaign was 90 percent up and running, running like a fine Swiss watch. There were only a couple more pieces missing. One of those final pieces necessary to further insure victory in what would more than likely be a close election was the position of secretary of state. Why, because the secretary of state was the individual who interpreted voting regulations and also the person who certified the vote after every election. This being the case whoever held that position could also quite possibly hold the key to victory in the 2000 presidential election.

The corporate-backed Republican machine was well aware of this. They were also aware of just how crucial it was that the person occupying that office was a dedicated Republican, willing to do anything, and I do mean anything necessary, to insure a George W. Bush victory in the upcoming presidential election.

This is where things get very interesting. From 1995 to 1999 a woman named Susan Mortham, a Republican, was Florida's secretary of state. Less than two years into her term a local business journal chronicled a string of embarrassing accusations against Ms. Mortham. None of the charges levied, at least at the time, appeared to diminish the support given to her by then-governor Bush or the Florida Republican Party. In August of 1998, Ms. Mortham announced that the current list of 18.2 million Florida voters contained at least 50,000 convicted felons and 18,000 dead people. At that time, she declared that she planned to make every effort possible to make sure those individuals dead or alive would not be able to vote during the September primary, a primary that was less than one month away.

A few days later, the August 19, 1998, issue of a popular and perceived by many as a very credible Florida newspaper reported that the Department of Justice in Washington, D.C., had instructed the secretary of state that her attempt to remove the names of felons from Florida's voter rolls was by federal law illegal. The Justice Department also notified the state that the new rules if enforced would more greatly impact black and Hispanic voters than white. Mortham said she disagreed with the Justice Department's decision that determined the new law would discriminate against minority races. She also stated that the Florida State Division of Elections would do its own research concerning the issue. Since there is no record of her ever doing so, I guess we have to conclude that Ms. Mortham never undertook such a study. About the same time this was going on, another very interesting situation materialized when the Florida State Association of Supervisors of Elections expressed their concerns in a private communication describing Ms. Mortham's apparent motiveless efforts, which if allowed to continue would result in the removal of a substantial number of names from the lists of Florida voters.

In what appears to me as her way of trying to legitimize her efforts, Ms. Mortham, in November of 1998, hired a private company, Database Technologies (now a subsidiary of Choice Point Inc.), to put together a list of Florida felons that if accepted by the Department of Justice in Washington would automatically have removed those names from the list of eligible voters, making them ineligible to vote in state primaries as well as all other Florida political elections. Around this time, while campaigning for office, Governor Bush cut all ties with Ms. Mortham. Now I'd like to inject a couple of questions that have puzzled me for quite some time. Why did it take approximately one year after the corruption in office allegations surfaced before Governor Bush decided to distance himself from Susan Mortham? One more intriguing question arose when, seemingly overnight, Governor Bush withdrew his support for Ms. Mortham and immediately backed a new candidate, Ms. Kathleen Harris.

Let's for one moment leave the realm of publicly recorded and/or published fact and enter the land of speculation and possibilities. From all the news stories I've read concerning Susan Mortham and her activities while secretary of state and because the ruling by the Justice Department made the implementation of her proposed list illegal, I have to assume that the list removing the names of felons was not in force during the September primary of 1998. I also have to conclude that since historically, blacks and Hispanics have for the most part always voted for Democratic candidates, the implementation of such a list would have only one purpose, and that was to give a huge advantage to the GOP, which in Florida at that time was the Republican Party, the party Susan Mortham belonged to.

Is it possible that some time shortly before Jeb Bush and the Republican Party cut Mortham loose, Governor Bush or a high-ranking member of George W. Bush's Republican campaign committee approached Ms. Mortham about using the now-infamous list during the 2000 election? If she refused their request it would easily explain why, as if overnight, her own party abandoned her. Now, as I mentioned at the beginning of this chapter, the 100 percent support of the Florida secretary of state would be crucial in a close election. That being the case, the Republican Party, as I mentioned earlier in this chapter, had to make sure that someone willing to do whatever had to be done in order to assure a Bush victory in 2000 occupied that office. Enter stage right, Ms. Kathleen Harris.

Let's learn a little bit more about Ms. Harris. Compliments of information acquired from various public sources. Ms. Harris graduated from high school in Bartow, Florida, in 1975. Three years later, she enrolled and began attending Spain's University of Madrid. That fact alone suggests that her family occupied a slightly higher tax bracket than the majority of us, which probably also places her family's political loyalties with the Republican Party. In 1979 she received a Bachelor of Arts degree in history with a specialization or second major in international trade and negotiations from Agnes Scott College in Decatur, Georgia. Then she went on to study under Christian theologian Francis Schaeffer at the L'Abri community in Huemoz, Switzerland. While attending college she also served as an intern for U.S. Representative Andy Ireland. In 1997 Harris also received a master's degree in public administration from Harvard University's Kennedy School of Government with a major in international trade.

Before entering politics Ms. Harris was employed as a marketing executive for IBM and a vice president of a commercial real estate firm. I've always said there's nothing like starting at or near the top.

Harris entered politics by winning election to the Florida Senate in 1994. Something I believe to be noteworthy is the fact that her campaign was one of the most expensive state races in Florida's history. Her quote unquote unknowing acceptance of illegal campaign donations made by a Sarasota-based Riscorp, Inc., and her subsequent sponsorship of a bill designed to block Riscorp competitors from getting a larger share of the

Florida workers' compensation market, not to mention her push for a proposal that would have hurt a particular competitor, only causes me to believe that her actions early in her political career pretty much brings to light the aggressive, no holds barred nature of Ms. Harris's character. In politics, more than in any other line of endeavor, the old saying "The end justifies the means" is not just an occasionally used method, it is thee method for achieving ones political goal. Let's face it. Ms. Harris was just what the Bush presidential campaign was looking for, and after defeating the incumbent candidate, Sandra Mortham, who had suddenly found herself up to her ears in corruption charges, the Harris win wasn't all that surprising.

Now, along with her new position as Florida secretary of state, Ms. Harris was given another high honor and responsibility, the co-chairmanship of George W. Bush's Florida campaign machine. OK, Mortham was out and Harris was in; sound familiar? From what I've been able to ascertain, the now-infamous voter exclusion list hadn't been implemented, at least not yet. Now in office, Kathleen Harris by decree hired a private firm called Choice Point. Remember that name? Their subsidiary was a company called Database Technologies, the same company Ms. Mortham was going to use to implement her plan to remove thousands of supposed felons and dead people from the voting rolls, that is, until the Justice Department stopped her. Choice Point's task still remained the same, and judging from the outcome of the 2000 election, I have to admit that they did their job extremely well. Their identification and removal of thousands of names from the state's voter's rolls, on the condition that these individuals were convicted felons, caused many of these people to be turned away at the polls or even before reaching the polls. It would, however, later be discovered that approximately 97 percent of those whose names were removed from the state voter rolls and were denied the right to vote in the presidential election were not felons at all. But in this election, maybe even equally as important as having their right to vote taken away was the fact that the majority of these voters were also African American, and as I mentioned before had traditionally been known to vote for a Democratic candidate. The situation created by the elimination of thousands of votes in the state of Florida soon brought about several investigations into the legitimacy of George W. Bush's 2000 election victory.

Before the ballots had a chance to cool, cries of outrage not to mention several threats of lawsuits filled the air. The news media, always loving the slightest hint of wrongdoing, answered the call, and within hours, every newspaper and news channel from coast to coast was headlining the story.

If there's one thing that has always set America apart from many other governed societies it's our right to free speech, guaranteed under the first amendment of our Constitution. I'm referring to the right to freely express our opinions. Since the Bush administration's rise to power, that first amendment right has in one way or another been threatened on more than one occasion. The one case that comes immediately to mind is the Valerie Plame affair.

I've always believed that the reason politicians in this country have pretty much always tolerated individuals or groups who loudly voice beliefs contrary to the establishments, whether vocally, in print, or both, is because they know the American voters much better than the voters know themselves. History has proven time and time again that in America, no matter how loud people scream or for what reason, Americans do not have the—let's see, how should I put this? OK, let's just say they lack the intestinal fortitude necessary to take the actions required to effect positive change. And much to the detriment of Americans, politicians realize this. OK, enough of that. Let's get back to Kathleen Harris's predicament.

Needless to say, within hours of the results, Kathleen Harris was flooded with allegations of conflict of interest and partisan and unethical behavior, none, or hardly any, of which was voiced without the use of certain adjectives that I will not include in this story for fear of having it receive an X rating. In the beginning, during, and even while the screams of wrongdoing continued, Kathleen Harris, unbending and resolute, remained true to her party and her mission by certifying the results giving George W. Bush the 2000 election and his victory over Al Gore. According to the official total number of votes cast. George W. Bush's win was by a mere 537 votes, which sounds more like the election results of a small town in upstate New York and not the entire state of Florida. Was the 2000 election fixed? I'll leave that conclusion up to you.

The Republican machine always rewards loyalty and a job well done. So for Ms. Harris's contribution to the

2000 presidential election they reciprocated by giving her their complete support during her next campaign bid, which was in 2002, when she ran for the U.S. House of Representatives in—can you imagine the luck—a heavily Republican district, a district where she won an easy victory. Ms. Harris next considered running in 2004 for the seat held by retiring Senator Bob Graham, but after discussing her future intentions with the Bush White House, she put her campaign plans on hold, apparently because the Bush administration had already reserved that seat for the up-and-coming secretary of housing and urban development, Mel Martinez. According to an article I read at the time, the Republican Party offered to support her 2006 election bid if she would stay out of the 2004 election. Ms. Harris agreed, and Mel Martinez ran for the seat and won. Thus began Mel's road to the White House. The rest is history.

Four years later, Ms. Harris announced her candidacy for the Florida seat in the U.S. Senate, challenging incumbent Bill Nelson. But due to her apparent inability to raise adequate campaign funds as compared to Bill Nelson's and a controversy created by a scandal concerning her campaign committee's fund-raising practices, with one company in particular named MZM, Harris fell far behind in the polls. However, Harris showed that she was still popular among Republican voters by winning the September primary over her opponent, a man named McBride. My question is this. What happened to all the support she was promised? Why did George W. Bush and his Republican Party, not to forget to include the president's brother, Jeb Bush, then the governor of Florida, dump Ms. Harris? I've always been curious to know who started the MZM, scandal in the first place. After observing politics through the years, I wouldn't be at all surprised if the White House provided the information that caused the accusations concerning the illegal campaign contributions. I guess it doesn't really matter who caused the situation. The damage was done. Little did Ms. Harris realize at the time that Mel Martinez, the individual she was asked to step aside for, was on his way up the political ladder, and Ms. Harris? Oh, she wasn't just on her way down. She was on her way out.

Now, let's check out the events that led to Ms. Harris's being abandoned by the party she'd done so much for. In May of 2006 Florida governor Jeb Bush questioned Harris's ability to win the upcoming election, encouraging others to run against her in the primary. Karl Rove—we all remember Karl, and it's not for his dancing ability— also expressed reservations concerning her ability to win. National Republicans criticized her campaign openly and in private and tried to convince other Republican candidates to run against Harris in the primary. Even President Bush, who relied on Ms. Harris so heavily during the 2000 election, now slammed the political door of opportunity in her face. Shortly after, Ms. Harris began firing campaign managers and staff members, the very people she had to have if she wanted any chance of winning the upcoming election. I believe it was at this time that she'd reached the end of the line. Her career in politics was in shreds, and finally came to a close in what can only be described as a total and complete meltdown.

The situation Ms. Harris found herself in is not unusual. Politics is the most brutal, no-holds-barred game on the face of this planet. Once in the game, you have no friends, only alliances, alliances that can and sometimes do change overnight. Everybody's figuring, and manipulating, twenty-six hours a day, eight days a week, and friends? A prominent politician once said if you want a friend in Washington, buy a dog. A truer statement has never been said. When a politician says the wrong thing or signs the wrong bill or supports the wrong candidate, any action that runs contrary to the current administration's policies or beliefs, if the powers to be feel the individual is no longer needed or can be of no further service. They automatically drop that individual like a hot potato. In politics, it isn't what have you done for me; it's what have you done for me today, or in some cases, even this minute. Those who are successful and remain in political life for any length of time constantly walk a tightrope. Even after years of showing their allegiance and devotion to their party, even going so far as to discard their own personal values, their honor, integrity, and beliefs, one fatal mistake, one refusal to go along, could very well mean the end of his or her career, or in the least, the end of their ability to climb higher on the crooked, slippery ladder of politics.

As a newly elected, young, and naive politician, you have two choices. You can jump headlong into the rotten apple barrel and mingle with the worms or get tossed out. If you find my statements hard to believe, I recommend that you ask Ms. Harris.

I think we all realize that life is full of coincidence. But as I mentioned more than once, at the beginning and a couple more times throughout this book, the events that transpire in politics never have and never will mirror the chance occurrences you and I occasionally encounter during our everyday life. Looking back at the events surrounding Sandra Mortham's loss of her party's support and her subsequent defeat to Kathleen Harris, all happening with the backing of what used to be Ms. Mortham's party, both occurring at just the right time is something I personally cannot accept as simply being an act of fate. But if you were to tell me it was the act of the devil or a manipulative group of politicians, now that statement I would find that a bit easier to believe.

All being said and done. Because of certain appointments to the Supreme Court by prior Republican presidents, appointments that would pretty much insure the outcome of certain cases, cases essential to the furthering of corporate America's policies and interests. One very important one being the decision that would determine the final outcome of the 2000 presidential election, which would guarantee the installation of G.W. and Dickey to the White House, was merely a formality or technicality. So after going through the mundane motion of obtaining a high court ruling, the Dick Cheney, George W. Bush AKA corporate America, came to power.

CHAPTER FIVE

Life under Dick and George

How's life been since our nation's hope was elected to office? Who has fared better, the working class or corporate America? I realize that according to a recent survey there is somewhere in the neighborhood of 27 percent of Americans polled who still consider the Bush administration's time in office as a tremendous success. If these statistics are accurate it only leads me to believe that the top 10 percent has grown a bit and the rest of those who still have favorable opinions toward the Bush administration probably never listen to the news, read newspapers or have been affected by the Bush corporate doctrine, or they've spent the last seven-plus years watching the cartoon channel.

There's no way I can recount or for that matter even know of all the wonderful things G.W. and associates have done for the American middle class. But let's see if I can list just a few. He passed a prescription drug plan about which one family of two said they'd be lucky if the plan saved them $25.00 a year. Not bad, right? Let's see, there was a tax decrease. How much did you save? How much did the upper 10 percent of our society save? And how about all those terrific jobs he's created in China? Oh, and don't forget the trade agreements that totally favor every nation on the planet except ours. I'll end my somewhat short list with his new and improved comprehensive immigration bill. It's not hard to understand just who really made out during the Bush reign. Although I guess, for approximately 27 percent of all those Americans poled, it apparently is.

Now, let's take a look at the other side of the coin. He made it harder for an employee to take his or her employer to court for wage or job advancement discrimination. Even though it hasn't been enforced, if my memory serves me, he was behind legislation making it illegal to buy less-expensive prescription drugs from Canada or Mexico while at the same time allowing China to import drugs used to make the final prescription drugs we pay so much for here, drug imports on a scale large enough to be used in at least 51 percent of America's prescription drugs.

He's not only allowed the continued operation and creation of monopolies, but I believe he showed his support by ignoring federal laws that were designed to control the operating and pricing practices of industries like big oil, to which in effect he has given the OK to continually raise oil and fuel prices at their discretion without necessary and truthful justification. I'd like to mention that the price of unleaded regular on the day George W. Bush entered the White House was $1.47 a gallon. What's it going for now? Look at today's pump price and add that to the $150 million in yearly tax breaks given to big oil and ask yourself these two questions. One, who's making a killing, and two, at whose expense? By the way, the Bush family has been involved in the oil business for decades. The same applies for drug companies and insurance providers. Funny, if my memory serves me correctly, those three industries, just to name a few, were all financial backers of his two presidential campaigns. For Wall Street's financial contributions he has been tirelessly trying to repay them by pushing legislation through Congress and the Senate that would turn over, at least for now, a small percentage of our Social Security checks to Wall Street investors. Don't sweat it! They'll get the rest later. Personally, I'd rather take the money and go to that little city in the Nevada desert where the odds of winning just might be a bit better. OK, now for our national parks. He's opened up thousands of acres for sale or for use by lumber and mining companies. From what I understand, he's done likewise for oil and natural gas exploration. He's advocated the sale of our ports to countries known to support terrorist organizations. He has allowed the prosecution of at least three border patrol agents for doing their jobs. He's done everything in his power to prevent the securing of our border with Mexico. He's totally in favor and pushing hard to pass a bill designed to give amnesty to between twelve and twenty million illegal aliens, which would also eventually lead to the total destruction of our Social Security system.

Medicare and Medicaid would soon follow. I read somewhere that he's already signed a bill that would give Social Security benefits to all illegal aliens who work in this country. He's committed to the removal of our borders and allowing free unrestricted travel throughout North America. In reality, George W. Bush is selling legislation, none of which is of his own design but has been carefully created by national and/or international corporate powers that for years have been steadily progressing toward their final goal of a global economy, which would in turn eventually end in the establishment of a one-world government. Their efforts to accomplish this goal can also be seen by observing the current rulings of the United States Supreme court that now appears to favor international law over laws set down in our own constitution. At present, George W. Bush's efforts to destroy America and its sovereignty are being referred to as the North American alliance of states. If this plan is allowed to become a reality, it would mean the end of ours, but apparently not his country. In other words, no more United States of America. He tells us that America's security would be stronger without borders. Does he believe that we're all a bunch of complete idiots? Granted, there are a bunch of them out there. Because of this I guess he has the right to believe it. After all, the voters did elect him, not once, but twice. In a world controlled by national and international corporate powers the welfare of the individual is not only un-important it is also a non-existent part of their overall equation. In today's America the will of the American people has also become un-important, a nuisance, only to be tolerated every four years. We have to wait that long before they come close enough to hear our cries for help.

Even then, once the election is over, they immediately forget the promises they made, knowing full well that the voters having extremely short memories will no doubt forget about those promises too. Four years later, he, or she can once again make the same promises. One promise I just have to mention. A promise that's used so often that it could be compared to an old worn out shoe. The one I'm referring to is the promise of change. In close to forty years of listening to election campaign rhetoric I've not once seen a campaign go by without the term being used, in at least a half dozen speeches given by politicians who promise to give it to us, and brother, do they ever. The only problem is what they give us is always negative, and more and more of the same. More jobs ex-ported, more illegal workers to replace Americans. More factories shut down, more and more Americans losing their homes, more increases in the cost of living. What can people do when their government stops listening, stops caring about them and about their country? If you were to take a brief look back through history you'd find at least two tragic events that occurred simply because governments turned their backs on their people.

As I believe I mentioned before, everything George W. Bush has done and will continue to do has one purpose and only one, to increase the power, control, and domination over America's workforce by the ever-growing corporate powers. His plan's success depends almost totally upon the elimination of America's borders and the inclusion of cheap labor. These two things must occur if corporate America's final objective is to be achieved.

Is George W. Bush's dream for the future, your dream? Is it mine? Unless you're a member of the board of directors of Exxon Mobil or are in the top 10 percent of America's wealthiest population, I hardly think so. Now, I'd like to ask a couple of probing questions. Just how much of our already dwindling personal freedoms are we all willing to give up in the name of George W. Bush's definition of security? Will the meager, half-hearted security measures he has already begun cutting funds for, once completely in place, protect the American people from the threat of terrorism? Or maybe they'll be needed to someday protect these corporate powers from the masses of the unemployed Americans and illegal aliens who have lost everything and now have nothing else to lose.

Any success the Bush administration has enjoyed during their two consecutive terms in office has come from the fact that the Democrats failed to field a viable candidate and through the application of two age-old political strategies. One, "A lie told once is still a lie. But a lie told again and again becomes the truth"; and two, the use of the fear strategy. It worked wonderfully after 9/11 and sure helped George in his 2004 reelection campaign. I'm not saying we do not have a serious threat facing us. Matter a fact I believe the threat is much greater than the Bush administration's reaction to it. Every step taken by George W. Bush since 9/11, every piece of legislation created by and/or backed by him and his until recently Republican-dominated Congress and Senate were created for several reasons, none of which has or will have anything to do with the security of our nation and everything to do with increasing corporate America's bottom line. Many of these bills were passed with special attention being paid to a number of privileged companies whose names can be found on the list pertaining to the Iraq war no-bid contracts. Each included in a scheme that I believe was created years earlier, possibly even before his first run for office. The actions of his administration have allowed corporate America the ability to increase their dominance over the working class by allowing them to raise the prices of consumer necessities to a level so high that in past times of natural disaster, anyone doing the same would have been accused of and likely prosecuted for price gouging. But under the Bush administration today's gouging is being allowed to continue without any interference what-so-ever from government regulatory agencies. In other words, the Bush administration has intentionally unleashed upon the American public a corporate monster whose appetite for profit and power can never and will never be satisfied. Every action taken by President Bush was, is, and I have to assume will in the future be the total opposite of that which would be taken by a president who truly has the security and welfare of his nation and its people foremost in his heart and mind. The only reasonable explanation I can possibly accept for his actions to date has to lie with his desire to increase the financial wealth of his political supporters, corporate America. When I look upon the face of George W. Bush or Dick Cheney, I see the truthfulness of a couple of used-car salesmen.

Talk is cheap, Mr. President, and each time you speak, the emptiness, deception, and lies continue to grow. I can see you, but I no longer hear your voice. We can sum up your administration's policies simply by saying that you, through Mr. Cheney, are the direct representative of big business, today's corporate powers who more than at any other time in the history of this nation makes each and every one of their decisions based entirely on the anticipation of the level of profits created by those decisions, each and every one completely void of compassion for the employees who will ultimately be affected by those decisions, all void of any feeling whatsoever for the death and destruction they through you Mr. President have caused during your time in office.

In order to maximize the profits that would be derived from any investment or undertaking, the war in Iraq being an extremely good example, only such actions designed to extend the length of time America remains involved will ever be implemented. Why? Because the longer the war continues, the more profit it will generate for the corporate entities that supply the goods and services, at what I might add are prices that should have been investigated years ago as not just being grossly inflated but also illegal. To say that Halliburton and others are raping the American taxpayer does not even come close to describing the unbelievably corrupt acts of thievery that began well before the first American soldier ever put his or her foot upon Iraqi soil, thievery that continues to go on in Iraq and at home. Simply put the election of George W. Bush in 2000 and again in 2004 amounted to nothing less than giving his political supporters a license to steal. There just isn't any other way to describe it.

If you were to view the war in Iraq and Afghanistan from the prospective of a member of the board of Halliburton then things are going great and couldn't be better. But if you're one of the thousands of badly wounded

American soldiers or the families of those soldiers who have given their lives or the surviving member or members of those who live in the two devastated countries of Iraq and Afghanistan, things couldn't get any worse.

Now I'd like to bring up the findings of a report I read a few months ago in which it stated that only fourteen cents of every dollar earmarked for Iraq ever gets there. Since the study and its findings were not top secret and published openly, I have to assume that the Bush administration knows of it. Yet, at least to my knowledge, not one word concerning this study has ever been discussed in public by anyone at the White House. Why? My own explanation is quite simple. The study was never and will never be discussed. No truthful investigation or actions taken as a result of such an investigation will ever take place. Why, because the White House knows exactly where a good portion of the missing eighty-six cents of every dollar is going.

I realize that as always, I'm jumping around a bit, but please bear with me while I leave the corruption behind. I'd like for a moment to discuss the make-up of our enemies in Iraq. There's always the fanatics the individuals who desire power and control. But they only make up a small percentage of the total opposition. A segment of their followers are also radicals but because of their lack of education, intelligence, and social skills. They are in- effective as leaders. Because of this they are forced to become followers. Both groups combined still only make up a small percentage of the overall total. Now, let's discuss those who make up the rest. When human beings lose everything—their loved ones, their homes, their jobs—when survival means having to scrounge through piles of garbage for something to eat, all this without any prospect of life getting any better, when death eventually appears to be more inviting than life, when all your life you've been taught of the glory of Allah and the paradise that awaits you, what would you do? Would you join an army that fights the infidels, the invaders? Would you consider becoming a suicide bomber? I wonder, how many suicide bombers has George W. Bush created?

The Bush-Cheney-Halliburton doctrine has had a significant effect on how the rest of the world feels towards America and Americans. To say that there are millions of people in other countries who dislike us and make up a world majority who feel the same might not be very far from the truth. I've talked to a couple people who were born and lived in Iraq. I was told that the Iraqi people blame us for what's going on in their country. Why, because we vote, and our government's actions represent the will of the American people. When I heard that, I nearly fell off my chair. Hell! The average American has zero representation at the county level. That being the case, how much of a voice could we possibly have on Capitol Hill? If we have one at all, it has to be about as powerful as a light early morning breeze and only felt every four years or so. Here's a small and I admit what may seem like a ridiculous example of our voice in government. In some parts of the county where my wife and I reside, the residents do not have the right to decide whether or not they want trash pickup. The county decided for them. They're even good enough to decide which company will be doing the picking up. If the company fails to make the agreed weekly pickup, sometimes for several weeks at a time, which has happened on more than one occasion the residents are still billed for the service they never received or in many cases never wanted. Oh, and if they refuse to pay, eventually, a lien will be placed against their property. Oh yeah, sure, we have a voice. Sorry, whenever I think about politics, garbage always comes to mind. And remember never take lightly the power wielded or the corruption that would be found if investigated at the county government level. By my way of thinking the county commission is the most powerful politically motivated branch of government in America, bar none. How can I make that statement? Think about it: What branch of government most directly controls and affects the lives of each and every one of us on a day-to-day basis? Ever so much more than state and federal government and considering that at least 90 percent of all the ordinances passed by county government, throughout this entire country, are unconstitutional. Early on, I have come to the conclusion that they are the power and there's nothing democratic about the way they use it. And freedom, what ever happened to the Bill of Rights? Were its amendments erased as part of a provision in one of George W. Bush's faith-based China trade agreements or maybe some port deal? Was it sold along with the Pennsylvania Turnpike? Maybe it was tacked on the end of the bill raising the minimum wage.

What can we the forgotten people expect in our future? Will a Democrat in the White House solve our problems? Don't hold your breath. According to an article I read in a very reliable magazine, the majority of financial backers who supported George W. Bush during his past two presidential campaigns, realizing that they've screwed the American people to such a degree that the reelection of a Republican candidate is highly unlikely, have switched their support to the Democratic front runner, Hillary Clinton, who as far as I'm concerned is a highly questionable candidate to begin with. And as you and I have found through past experience, once the less of two evils enters office and we find that we've elected the wrong one, as in the case of George W. Bush, payback is a bitch. Oh no! Not for George or Hillary or whoever wins the next presidential election, but for us, you and I. The old slogan "the buck stops here" is definitely true. But these days it doesn't stop at the Oval office. Why, because you and I, and not G W Bush, are the ones who feel the effects of every piece of bad legislation that becomes law. Let's face it the buck really stops with the American people. Let's take a look at a couple of our presidential hopefuls. How about Bill Richardson? He's in favor of dissolving our borders. He and Hillary are also supporters of the new and improved comprehensive immigration bill. Mr. Giuliani has a contract with the tiny Persian Gulf Kingdom of Qatar. In other words, big oil, if that doesn't ring a bell in your head. Let me give you a clue. The Bush family had and probably still has contracts and close personal ties with the Saudi royal family. Could that be the reason Saudi Arabia has been given the hands-off treatment? Could it have any bearing on why our fuel prices have more than doubled since George Jr. entered the White House? If Mr. Giuliani was still in the race and won the presidential election in 2008 could we expect the same relationship and favored treatment for a nation that financially supports the building of schools that teach hatred for the west, the same country from which the majority of the 9/11 hijackers came? I won't continue to dwell on the flaws each candidate possesses, flaws caused by the fact that each one is owned by big money and special interest groups, but believe me, they all have them. Oh, and before you vote for any one of this year's presidential candidates, do yourself a favor. Take a few minutes and briefly look into where their campaign donations came from. Because when you cast your vote this November, you're not voting for a candidate. You're casting your vote for the corporations that supported their political campaigns. One of which is undoubtedly Exxon Mobil.

There's one thing I can assure you. Not one of the candidates running for the nomination has achieved the political positions and endorsements that have allowed them to run for the presidency because of what he or she has done for working-class Americans. Take a look at John Edwards. Last time around he not only failed to win his state but couldn't even carry the precinct where he lived. In other words, his neighbors didn't like him, but we're supposed to. In politics, there's no profit to be derived from helping the working class. Why, because working class men and women cannot compete financially with the thousands of corporate lobbyists who on any given day in one way or another are presenting incentives or more accurately stated, bribing the people we elected to support us. The average American can't afford to continually pay their political representatives each and every time they want them to do what he or she was elected to do and is already being paid to do. As average wage earners we cannot afford to send our politicians to the Bahamas for a two-week fact-finding tour or loan them a private jet. Everyday working people are not in a position that would enable them to open an offshore bank account for themselves, let alone anyone else. No, the best a politician can hope to do if he or she wants to win reelection is to treat their constituents the same way a farmer grows his mushrooms. In other words keep them in the dark, and feeding them a whole lot of manure. Remember the saying "you can fool all the people some of the time and some of the people all the time but you can't fool all the people all of the time?" For the last god only knows how many years, at least for corporate America's representatives on capitol hill and in the White House it appears to me that its been very easy to fool all the people all of the time.

So when you go to the polls this coming November, keep in mind that you're not voting for the best candidate. You'll be trying to do what all of us have been attempting to do for years now, trying to pick the lesser of two evils, and considering our track record and the direction our nation's been going, I'm not so sure that a lesser even exists.

I'd like to now quote, as accurately as I can, two phrases written somewhere within the pages of the St. James Bible. Doing so even for fear of upsetting a segment of our society that hates to even see a copy of the Ten Commandments hanging anywhere except maybe on the back wall of some dark and very remote closet: Well, here goes. "The flesh is weak" and "Money is the root of all evil." You know, come to think of it, I can't remember if I read those in the St. James or heard it used as an excuse by one of the numerous male politicians who every year or so gets caught trying to engage in deviate sexual practices with the guy sitting in the next bathroom stall. That or finds himself apprehended with both hands and feet in the taxpayers' cookie jar.

CHAPTER SIX

The Politics of Open Border Immigration

Who benefits from so-called comprehensive immigration reform? And why reform at all when immigration laws have been on the books for years? I'd like to discuss this as it relates to middle-class America's future under the final solution. But before delving into this topic, I'd like to say that in my experience, whenever government uses words like overhaul or comprehensive in connection with any program that was originally designed to benefit the taxpayer, it always means the taxpayers are about to be exposed to another round of anal intercourse, and worse yet, our, excuse me, their representatives never forget to bring along the sand. I suppose a nicer way of putting it would be that we end up holding the very dirty end of a short stick. But maybe it's time the American people dispensed with the niceties and told these despicable individuals exactly what they really think. As it currently stands, whenever government overhauls any program, it means more corruption, more overspending, and shrinking benefits for the American taxpayer. Oh, and quite possibly more bennies for illegal aliens, one of many, many examples being the $10 million that the current corporate Congress just set aside for ambulance chasers, excuse me, lawyers, so they can defend the rights of people who aren't supposed to be in this country in the first place. But no matter what the results of government involvement may initially be, for us it always means exactly the same thing. The wealthy, the minority groups, the individuals who are not supposed be in this country, companies that employ illegal, cheap labor, and politicians who support legislation that creates these overhaul programs always benefit at the expense of you and I.

I realize that you probably already know the answer to the question of open border immigration. But please stay with me and just maybe we'll uncover a couple of less obvious reasons behind George W. Bush's tireless efforts to make this particular piece of legislation the law of the land.

Corporate America has used every means available to cut operating expenses, except, that is, to get people to work for nothing or maybe even pay the companies they work for just for giving them the opportunity to do so. In our current-day corpocracy, the list of cost-cutting options is growing very short. Today, the move that would bring about the most profit in the shortest amount of time would come from you guessed it, the flood of illegal aliens, the influx of which has already caused wages in several job areas of America to fall like a rock. Once the corporate America's comprehensive immigration bill becomes law, and believe me, it will, whether bits and pieces of it are tacked on page 4,025, paragraph "C," sub-chapter "S," in the third edition, volume 35, or passed as one piece of legislation whose reworking and recreation has been praised throughout the hallowed halls of Congress by corrupt politicians as being the best thing that's happened since Roosevelt's New Deal. Even if the people refuse to buy it, even with the tremendous numbers of Americans being against it, some day it will become a reality. Why? Because corporate America wants it; that's why! When that day comes, cheap labor will flood this country like never before, along with zero workplace health and safety standards. Eventually, both will become the accepted norm in the workplace. Oh, we won't like it, and I'm sure some will demonstrate and others naive enough to still believe that those they've elected to political office actually represent them will contact those representatives, all in a futile attempt to urge them to do what they were elected to do in the first place. But if you truly believe our, excuse me, their politicians really give a damn about the problems we the people have, then you're probably among the same number of Americans who still attempt to stay awake every Christmas Eve trying to get a glimpse of Santa laying out the toys under the tree. Let's face it, without the bargaining power of unions, without political representation, without Americans who have the honesty, integrity, and intestinal fortitude of our forefathers, in plain English the balls necessary to turn the tide of rampant corruption, we'll have to continue doing exactly what we've been doing for years now: accept it.

Will passage of the new and improved comprehensive immigration bill put an end to the flood of illegal aliens entering this country? Our president and his supporters have said it will. But come on, get real! You and I know it won't even slow them down. If anything, their numbers will increase in hopes of being able to catch a ride on comprehensive immigration reform bill number three, and now, I'll let you in on a secret: G.W. and friends know it too.

Each and every piece of legislation ever passed for the purpose of creating laws in order to govern a nation and/or provide adequate security for that nation never achieved their intended purpose unless those laws were enforced. We could have reduced the problem of illegal border crossings to a trickle years ago. Why didn't we? Because years ago, the politicians that the American voters placed their trust in by electing them to political office jumped on the corporate-funded gravy train by siding with big money instead of supporting legislation that was in the best interests of America and the voters who gave them their overpaid jobs. In return, politicians from all branches of government, right from Capitol Hill and the Oval Office to the lowly county commissions throughout this country, began receiving the extras, the perks that only officials elected to public office have the opportunity to enjoy—extras like campaign donations, skiing trips to Aspen, or maybe two weeks in Aruba; free lunches and dinners at a popular D.C., hangout, a place I've been told where a constituent would have more luck finding his or her representative than by going to their office on Capitol Hill; promises of future employment as lobbyists from the companies they continually passed legislation for; and let's not forget the probability of unknown amounts of undeclared and well-hidden cash. Oh yes, from the very beginnings of American government, when any politician was in a position to help big money and did, they were very well paid for their efforts.

As I see it, the only difference between the corruption of yesteryear and that of today lies in the amount of the bribe and in the openness with which those in places of power carry out their shameful and treasonous activities. When these so-called representatives of the people accepted their first bribe, on that day they turned their backs on all of us who trusted them to maintain our nation's security and protect our way of life—what we're seeing today is the result of what began many, many years ago.

To understand one more reason George W. Bush has been pushing this amnesty legislation, we have to go back a couple of years and look at his new and improved comprehensive Wall Street Social Security overhaul program. Remember when he informed the American people that the Social Security system would be bankrupt within I believe the number was twenty years? Maybe if the federal government stopped using our retirement fund as their own personal piggy bank and also stopped giving Social Security benefits to people who do not deserve them, which now also includes who knows how many thousands of illegal aliens, Maybe, just maybe the impending SSI disaster we're continually being reminded of would not exist or at least not be as disastrous as we're told.

Putting that aside, President Bush's solution was to allow each retiree (I believe force would eventually be a better term) to invest a portion of his or her SSI retirement check in the stock market. In order to make the possibility of his grand Social Security plan more of a necessary step rather than an option. A year or so later he signed a bill that allowed a segment of illegal aliens to collect some form of SSI benefits.

Well folks, G.W. didn't wake up one morning and like a lightning bolt out of the blue, come up with the idea. No sir! A few months, maybe even a year prior to publicly announcing his new and improved plan to America. He was visited by a small group of very powerful individuals from Wall Street. By the time the motley crew left the Oval Office, Rose Garden, or wherever he gets together with his political supporters in order to hammer out the dents and put the final touches on any piece of garbage he believes he can shove down the public's throat. The finished product, as he likes to refer to pretty much every piece of legislation, came to life as the new comprehensive Social Security fix-all plan. I truly believe that just as the majority of federal pilot programs begin as being temporary, this too would eventually become what it's really intended to be, a permanent Wall Street bailout at the expense of America's future senior citizens; billions of dollars invested without the probability of ever receiving the kind of adequate return that would make it worth the investment, but with a more than average chance of incurring substantial losses.

The federal government has a long history of squandering billions, no trillions, of American tax dollars. They can't find enough toilets to flush it down or pockets to put it in. They spend it like it's flowing from a horn of plenty, and they sure as hell don't spend it like it's theirs. Why? Because it's not theirs—it's yours and mine. At least it was until they got their pudgy little sweaty hands on it. I can never say enough about the guardians of our nation and our tax dollars, all of which is well deserved and extremely uncomplimentary. If you were to harbor the worst possible thoughts concerning politicians, you'd probably have a 99.9 percent chance of being accurate.

Remember Enron, and a half dozen other large corporations who were caught using what was later referred to as "Creative Bookkeeping 101"? George W. Bush's SSI program was not designed to lend a helping hand to all of us current and eventually to be old folks who some day will need it but will very likely not see a dime of it. It was conjured up in order to pump billions of taxpayer dollars into a shaky stock market made that way because of corrupt company executives whose actions resulted in a loss of public confidence, a situation created by companies like Enron. And guess what—millions of dollars from Bush's SSI wall street bailout program could very well end up in the bank accounts of Enron, which, by the way, is still in business, when in a just society its board of directors would now be serving long prison terms. Let's not forget the other corporations who would benefit from the influx of SSI dollars, companies who on any given day could very well end up on the front page of the *Times* or other nationally syndicated newspapers.

As I mentioned above, George W. Bush's plan would no doubt begin as voluntary. But once his Immigration

Bill became law twenty million plus illegal aliens would automatically become legal residents and by so doing be entitled to certain Social Security benefits. When that occurs, it will, as President Bush fully realizes, make his Social Security plan no longer just an option, but a necessity, and for the American people, a very grim reality. Why? Because Social Security will go broke under the strain of providing benefits to an overwhelming population of illegal aliens who would automatically become legal and eligible for benefits, benefits created for the American people, benefits I sincerely believe illegal immigrants do not deserve. The final outcome would be a win-win situation for Wall Street, and corporate America's men in the White House would have successfully killed two birds with one stone. How can I say this? Because the American people would no longer have any choice but to accept the president's plan, and the effects of its passage into law would be disastrous. I believe that within a relatively short period of time. I'd guess within three years, the wages in America would begin a rapid descent to a level that resembled those of a third-world nation. Bush's plan would, as I mentioned above, become mandatory and permanent, and no matter how you slice or dice it, millions of new recipients would soon consume every dollar we, not they, contributed to the SSI fund. End result: bankruptcy for the system, while Wall Street walks away smiling. That's right; the passage of the comprehensive immigration fix-all bill number two will mean the quick and complete demise of not only SSI, but also Medicare, Medicaid, and many other federally funded social programs that will be overwhelmed by millions upon millions of new eligible recipients . As I mentioned before, this will also mean the addition of at least thirteen to twenty-plus million workers to the U.S. labor pool, giving America's present workforce a very destructive shot in the arm by millions of people willing to work for rock-bottom wages. This situation, to the overwhelming joy of corporate America, will continue to drive wages down for everyone.

Our new American non-citizen citizens will also be voters and as such will have their voices heard. I'm sure that when they go to the poles, their voices will be heard, and as has been the case for many, many years now, ours will continue to be ignored. America will have a new and strong block of voters who would eventually push legislation in a direction favoring the agendas they support, such as open borders, and away from legislation that would benefit a good percentage of legal immigrants, naturalized citizens, and those of us whose families have been here for hundreds of years. Overnight, America's majority would become America's new minority.

The passage of a bill that gives amnesty to twenty million illegal aliens who will become eligible to vote will also mean a labor-voter explosion. Both events easily explain why both Democrats and Republicans climbed on board in support of the new and improved comprehensive immigration bill. The Democrats want the votes, and the Bush administration would have achieved one more in the number of goals that George W. Bush probably agreed to when accepting financial support from America's corporate sector, one of those I'm sure being the endless supply of cheap labor in order to boost corporate America's yearly profits.

Both parties have everything to gain and nothing to lose. When the game of politics in Washington comes to an end, the game that plays hardball with all our lives and determines how Americans will live and sometimes even where they will live, the final score is always the same: corporate America's government fifty, the American people zip. When I think about America's disintegrating labor and economic situation, it always reminds me of a paper bag that's just about empty. As any of us who have ever gone to the market knows, a bag that's full is quite strong and pretty solid. But take all the contents out of that bag and it doesn't take very much force to collapse it. The bag I'm referring to signifies America, a nation that used to be filled with millions upon millions of American jobs, decent-paying jobs, jobs that were done by Americans.

Taking a quick look at the two politicians who created the comprehensive immigration bill and the president who supported it, I have to say that when a loose-cannon liberal like Senator Edward Kennedy comes up with or supports a piece of legislation, the blood in the veins of all working middle-class Americans should begin to run cold, and as far as Senator John McCain goes, let me tell you a short story concerning Senator McCain, one that occurred a few years back. All through John McCain's political career, although being a staunch die-hard Republican at heart, he's always voiced his own opinion. He was his own man. He spoke his own mind even if it left him at odds with the power brokers of the past and present administrations. During the early years of the Bush-Cheney administration's first term, Senator McCain joined and in some cases even led Senate opposition to some of George W Bush's policies. Because of this Senator McCain's was excluded from all White House social and political functions. Then, as if someone had turned on a light switch, McCain began supporting President Bush. Not on one or two issues, but on every issue. It wasn't long after that before he was back in the good graces of G.W. and the White House staff, and once again Senator McCain's name was added to the White House RSVP mailing list.

What caused Senator McCain's overnight transition from representative of the people to a yes man willing to bend to the will of President Bush and company? I believe he was told point blank by those who wield the political power in the Republican Party that if he ever wanted to achieve or even attempt to achieve the office of the presidency, he had to make one of the most important decisions of his life, a decision that would ultimately decide his political future. He could continue to support the best interests of the American people and never pick up the support of the Republican Party or he could abandon his principles and his beliefs and support George W. Bush's agenda. A quick look at his voting record for the last couple of years indicates, at least to me, that he chose the latter. When he did this, I believe he lost thousands of votes and the respect and confidence of millions of Americans, me included. Of course, since the attention span of the average voter is I believe the equivalent of a three-year-old, Senator McCain might just still have a chance.

But getting back to the Kennedy-Bush alliance, when corporate America's George W. Bush and a Massachusetts liberal like Senator Kennedy climb on board the same bandwagon, then it's time for the rest of us to firmly place at least one hand over the pocket that contains our wallet and, without hesitation, jump the hell off.

Over the years, I've become extremely suspicious of anyone who uses words like Hallelujah or praise the Lord or continually uses the Lord's name in every other sentence or as the main focal point of every conversation. If you ever meet a person who displays the tendencies I've just mentioned, remember, this is an individual you should never, never turn your back on.

Remember the glory days of the Bush administration? The early days when we didn't know, although we should have, what he and Exxon Mobile, Halliburton, and quite possibly the Saudi royal family, just to name a few of his many cronies, were up to? The days when we believed every word that came out of his Christian mouth? When we the people pinned all our hopes on this guy from Texas, a time when George W. Bush appeared to espouse the characteristics that most of us attribute to an individual who is an honest-to-God Christian? A person who took religion seriously and lived by the teachings of our Lord? Funny thing though. I've read quite a few pages in the St. James Bible, I never saw a passage that said, " Thou shall Lie, cheat, and screw thy people." Maybe I accidentally missed a page or two.

Remember the months, weeks, and days leading up to the 2000 election, when the Republican Party, in dire need of the vast number of votes held by the religious right, appeared to experience a tremendous and instantaneous religious transformation? Almost like the one

Ebenezer Scrooge was subjected to, the only difference being that Ebenezer's, was real and took hold. Where, as in the case of the Republican Party who has the ability to turn their love for our Lord and his teachings on and off, it was definitely not.

In those days, the Republicans couldn't say enough about the Lord God. The halleluiahs and praise the Lord's were flying all over the place. At the time they made me feel downright ashamed of myself for not being as good a Christian as they were.

Well, don't feel too bad about being duped. After all, George Jr. and Dickey fooled all of us, even the Religious Right. I was going to say even the Congress and Senate. But considering that both branches of government have shown us time and time again that as far as their ability or rather their inability to competently deal with America's problems, I have to believe they are overflowing with incompetent fools or a nationwide collection of village idiots. This being the case, I decided not to use them as examples. Listen people! If we're all trying to rid our communities of our local village idiots by sending them to Washington, we have to stop it. We have to stop it right now.

I've found, more times than not, that those who overuse the name of the Lord are usually employed as part-time self-ordained preachers and full-time used-car salesmen. Of course, as in everything, there's always an exception to the rule. In this case, the exceptions usually end up as residents of one of our nation's prisons or, if able to successfully elude the law, they go through life working confidence rackets or as politicians. Those individuals running in the pack who possess excellent memories and the gift of gab along with the ability to shovel the right kind and amount of shit and let's not forget being able to discard their principles along with their consciences have an excellent chance of moving up the political ladder. For these men and women, the sky's the limit, maybe even the presidency. But for the rest, whose memories among the other characteristics or traits I mentioned above are not as sharp or quick to change, well, they have to be content with lower positions in government such as senators or congressmen. And those whose memories are most deficient, well sadly, they have to accept the lowly positions reserved for county commissioners.

Even though winning election to any of these offices does require a certain amount of oratorical ability, once the election is over, there's only one rule that every politician must follow. I believe I mentioned it a couple chapters ago. It's called the "treat the people like mushrooms rule." In other words, keep 'um in the dark and feed 'um a lot of shit, and believe me, they never would have won any election if they didn't have the ability to do both and do it well.

Now, let's move on to a very, very serious subject. If this nation remains on its current path, I sincerely believe that the following events will move from the realm of fiction to that of reality. Just in case you might have missed one of life's most important lessons while growing up, I'd like to state it right now in a very condensed version: "Nothing in life ever comes without a price; nothing." Unfortunately, when government is involved the price is always paid by the poor and the ordinary working class, people like you and me. Men and women who pretty much live from paycheck to paycheck. On the other hand, those who belong to the upper financial segment of our society generally have enough investments and capital to insulate themselves against the harsh realities that we the people, or should I say we the forgotten people, have to deal with pretty much on a daily basis.

In the not-too-distant future, the greatest problem facing corporate America will also be its most challenging. I'm referring to the balancing act of trying to maintain a large enough international buying public needed to support the continuation of corporate America's ever-increasing yearly projected earnings. I also believe that eventually these mega-corporations will be forced to move the majority of their product lines, at least here in America, away from the manufacture of luxury products, replacing them with goods and services that make up the basic necessities of life. Why? Because eventually, sales of homes, automobiles, recreational vehicles, and all big-ticket luxury items, not to mention vacations, visits to theme parks, and even dining out, will become a much more rare occasion for all but the smallest segment of American society. This growing trend will quickly impact all who are involved in the process of providing these products and services. Bankruptcies throughout this country will increase as never before seen since 1929. Once this final economic breakdown begins in earnest, the destruction of the middle class will be well on its way and irreversible; that is, until a complete meltdown causes America's economy to bottom out. This event, as disastrous as it will certainly be is the only way that the destructive effects brought on by years of government corruption and corporate control can be ended, slowed or at least temporarily reversed. When the bottoming out or depression hits. American industry, what there is left of it, will be destroyed. Americans will begin experiencing years of extreme social unrest and economic hardship that if you can possibly imagine it will be much more devastating than the depression of 1929. Only in this way can a new cycle of economic growth begin again. The above scenario does not have to become a reality. Time is short but through swift legislative action by dedicated hardworking, elected officials in Washington. Our nation's future can be changed. Action in the form of legislation aimed at creating jobs for "Americans." Not just jobs, but decent-paying jobs, American jobs that could once again become a reality if government regulation of the major industries was again enforced. Only through fair and equally profitable trade agreements will we ever see the rebirth of American industry and American middle class prosperity. I sincerely believe that the two ways I just mentioned above could give our country a good start back on the road to recovery, a road that would once again stimulate the U.S economy bringing wages, and the cost of goods back in line. Our only problem lies in just where we'll find legislators like the ones I described, surely not on Capitol Hill.

How can any positive change be possible when the federal government's policies toward the operating practices of big business have been drafted by the heads of or representatives of large corporations, every policy totally favors not the American worker, but big business. Let's face the facts. Today, any regulations dealing with corporate America's employment and operating policies are nothing more than smoke and mirrors and amount to nothing in the way of real enforcement or restriction. Present-day American corporations, especially the largest of them, operate without any true regulation or legitimate oversight what-so-ever. If this situation, along with open border policies and trade agreements that totally favor China, Mexico, Japan, and others are allowed to continue, the inevitable meltdown I described will indeed become reality. The following is a more detailed description of what I predict America's future to be.

Because every business failure directly or indirectly impacts a number of other businesses and the people working in them, a downward spiral or, as some might refer to it, a domino effect will begin, eventually resulting in widespread economic disaster. From that time on, and for a number of years to follow, life in America will in many ways resemble that of the late twenties and thirties. But because of the tremendous increase in population and our over-dependence on foreign imports, this time around, as I stated previously, it will be much worse.

Along with the ever-increasing number of bankruptcies nationwide, basic necessities, items the general population needs to exist. Because of shortages in supply of those necessary goods, whether real or man-made, Americans will be exposed to an endless stream of steadily rising prices. Because of massive unemployment, very low wages, and inflationary prices, a large black market will soon emerge. This situation will continue to grow at an alarming rate and will for the most part become unstoppable as long as it continues to be fueled by the steady decline in wages and diminished employment opportunities all brought about by a corporate controlled government which supports the heavy influx of super-cheap illegal, legal immigrant labor along with the continued exportation of American middle class jobs.

Americans, even individuals with college-level educations, including those who hold two or more degrees, will find themselves competing with America's new illegal, legal citizens, people who are willing to work for a lot less than we can afford to. Corporate America will finally have arrived at the point they've been working toward for so many years, the complete domination of the workforce in order to create maximum profit. Our new citizens, who live together sometimes ten, twelve, or more in accommodations originally designed to house a family of four, will force Americans to make tremendous readjustments in their own lifestyles in order to compete with the demands of an ever-changing job market. In other words, our quality of life will become substantially lower and eventually resemble the societies of third-world nations. Long before this occurs, Social Security benefits will have disappeared, only to become just another payroll tax.

Quality healthcare, as it is today, will be limited to those who can afford it, the only difference being the number of those who can.

Individual ownership of homes, at least for the majority, will eventually become a thing of the past, as government-subsidized, low-income, welfare-like projects, similar to those found today in large cities like Chicago and New York, become the new homes for the most fortunate members of the fastest-growing population in America, a population that will consist of our new illegal, legal immigrants and the middle class American worker and his family. Gas and oil prices, the cost of living, along with the cost of purchasing and maintaining a vehicle will eventually cause such a great decline in American new and used-car sales that the majority of car manufactures will be forced to close their doors, leaving the building and sales of America's automobiles to countries like China, South Korea, and Japan along with a very small number of specialized American shops that cater to the rich. The closing of America's auto industry will add thousands of additional Americans to an already staggering number of unemployed.

What will replace the automobile as the mode of transportation? There are only a couple of options left for the average American: walking, mass transit, and of course, the bicycle. People residing in rural areas fortunate enough to be employed will be forced to move as close as possible to their places of employment. The return of company-owned row houses again lining the streets outside the factory gates could once again become a reality

Taxes on the working class will consume the greater portion of each person's paycheck. Why? Because as Leona Helmsley once said, "Only the little people pay taxes," and guess what category most of us belong to? Let's face it. The federal income tax short form wasn't created for the Rockefellers of America. And hell, someone has to pay for the hundreds, no thousands of new prisons and law-enforcement jobs that will have to be created as the size of North America's new and comprehensive poor population keeps growing. Let's not leave out the ever-expanding size of government, a government that as time continues will have to keep an ever-increasingly watchful eye on its citizens. Why? Because history has proven time and time again that as poverty increases, so does crime. Because of the level of poverty created by America's by then well-established corpocracy, law-enforcement agencies of the future will have to be colossal in size and number in order to control the greater segment of the population who has been forced to turn to crime because they can no longer survive without doing so. This level will be at least ten times the current national average and growing. What would you be willing to do in order to feed your family?

The events, I just described above could easily be the basis for a Hollywood movie but as most of us who are old enough to remember Flash Gordon or Dick Tracy, know, fiction somehow has a strange way of becoming reality. But it doesn't have to. Or does it? Can we change our course, man's course? Has greed being one of his strongest traits already pre-determined our fate?

The future of America will be bleak to say the least if we remain on the path our—excuse me, I never refer to them as my or our representatives because they are nei-ther—but as I was saying, if we remain on the path they have chosen for us. Sadly, nothing short of an armed na-tional rebellion in which as always, we the people would lose or a tremendous, honest to goodness religious awak-ening by the corrupt individuals we're stupid enough to keep electing will America have any chance at all of returning to the days when it was everyone's country and not just corporate America's and the top 10 percent, when it was the nation that lit the way for all who dreamed of truth, justice, freedom, and democracy. Those days are gone now. Why? Because of our laziness, our indifference, or our refusal to hold the people we elect accountable, truly accountable. For these reasons, we've allowed them to take away many of our rights, and also to take our nation away from us. Is what we're facing today and will face in the future just a sign of the times and the natural regression or disintegration of a civilization heading for total and complete destruction? Is it the natural, historically proven process brought about because of man's corrupt nature? A characteristic common to all human beings since the Garden of Eden, the very same deadly imperfection that has brought about the end of so many other great societies of the past? Or is it, in truth, the final signs leading to the end of America, the harsh of retributions for allowing the creation of such times, because we have surely done that.

Modern-day society looks down upon the virtues our forefathers taught or tried to teach us, traits our founding fathers possessed that enabled them to fight and many, oh so many times, caused them to give their lives in order that future generations would have this special place on Earth called America; a place where people could live, work, and practice their religious beliefs free from oppression; a country where all its citizens were allowed to dream and make those dreams come true. All this made possible by people who held certain ideals above personal gain, things like honesty, integrity, honor, loyalty. Today, all these virtues are looked down upon and considered ridiculous, out of date, old fashioned, or obstacles to success. These feelings are not only held by a large majority of the general public but also by America's leaders who depend on lies, deception, and half truths to succeed in furthering their own corrupt agendas, policies that have nothing to do with improving or maintaining our way of life but quite the opposite.

Democracy cannot hope to survive without the continual participation of its people. Throughout the years, we've seen and felt the consequences that occur when we put our trust in others and walk away. Time and time again we've seen what happens when corporate powers send lobbyists whose pockets are bulging with money, money used to buy the support of individuals in whom we the people by electing them to office have placed our trust, a trust that they will safeguard our nation, our way of life, our future, and the future of our children. These individuals, void of conscience, who are supposed to be our representatives have long ago deserted us. This latest piece of traitorous immigration legislation is just one more nail in the coffin of not just every working American, but in America itself.

This last chapter discussed several issues including its main topic, which describes just a few of those who will benefit greatly from illegal, legal immigration. Understandably, if we listed all of them, the list would be extremely long. But, as always, the American people didn't make that list they never had a chance. Why, because in today's corporate-controlled government, the needs of the American people are not even considered a minor priority.

CHAPTER SEVEN

America, the Debtor Nation, and its Leaders

As hard as it may be for most of us to believe, at one time, America stood tall and independent. We were able to do this because we owed no one. Our factories hummed with the sounds of progress, prosperity, and employment for all who wanted to work. Over the years, because of national and international corporate-profit-oriented policies supported by their two main philosophies, referred to as "greed is good" and "expand or die," skyrocketing and seemingly endless profits made from essential products and services such as oil, insurance, and pharmaceuticals being sold to the public, all at prices that under other circumstances such as natural disasters would be considered price gouging, have done more to directly affect and control the quality of life for the average working American than any other action or actions allowed not only to continue, but to flourish under the auspices of government support. The day big business signed its first trade agreement or placed its first order with an overseas company, that was the day they began selling out our nation and the future of the American people, all in the name of profit. All in the name of greed they sold our future and the future of endless generations of the yet unborn Americans, all to the lowest bidder.

Now let's get to the topic of this chapter. The same cause and effects of borrowing as it relates to an individual or average family also applies to a corporation and yes, even to a nation's government. The size of the budget involved and the amount of money involved are both irrelevant. The basic principles governing spending and balancing one's budget always remains the same. One bedrock solid fact of life is that the more you spend, the less you have. Simple, isn't it? Any of us who've had credit cards, which is probably all of us and then some, know where I'm headed.

Let's break it down to an easily understood, laid-back budget situation by discussing a guy on the street. Let's call him Joe Smith. Joe has a pretty good job. But like most of us, his monthly bills leave very little left over for the extras he would like to have. You know, the things that make life worthwhile. One day Joe opened his mailbox, and saints preserve us, he found the answer to his prayers: two dozen applications for credit cards. At last he could buy that new motorcycle and maybe even a big-screen TV. The monthly payments wouldn't be a problem, at least most months, and even if he was a little short, he could always juggle his bills. You know, let one slide a week or so and then pay it a little late; no problem.

First of all, as soon as Joe or our nation began borrowing, whoever the lenders are, whether ABC credit or China, some outside power has begun dictating or controlling at least to some degree a portion of Joe's life or as in the case of a nation, its trade or maybe its immigration policies. If Joe misses his monthly payment, maybe the credit card company will raise his rates, and poor Joe? He has no choice but to pay the increase. Nations that lend millions or billions as in the case of America's policy of borrowing from China and other countries have now been given the leverage they need to demand, in a casual, diplomatic way of course, certain trade benefits or maybe access to some of our weapons technology, or how about visas for more of their people, visas that allow certain individuals to enter and leave the United States with a minimum, if any at all, amount of investigation or hassle. How about their now having the ability to secure contracts that would allow them to supply our major food companies with all sorts of goods, 99 percent of which never see any inspection at all. How about the food we feed our pets, and let's not forget pharmaceutical drugs that when combined with others make up our finished prescription drugs, which, by the way, account for over 50 percent of all prescription drugs sold in America or how about toys for our kids? You know, the toys covered with paint containing high amounts of lead. Because of the tremendous amount of imports that we receive from countries like China we are now unable to say no. How can we? If we did, they could and probably would cut off the funds we need to keep our government's outrageous over-the-top spending spree going, you know, just as the credit card company could stop Joe's ability to maintain his now slightly upscale lifestyle. And even worse, in both cases, each could demand immediate repayment of the money borrowed.

In the case of the U.S. government, the geniuses who run this country, or more accurately put, have run this country into the ground, aren't worried. Why? Because just like so many administrations before them, in order to keep borrowing more and more, they just borrow that more from Peter in order to pay Paul. I guess we've all been guilty of doing that at one time or another. And I guess we also know what eventually happens if we allow it to continue: bankruptcy all around. You see, unlike Joe, who has no one to pass his debt onto, the politicians in Washington, even on the state and county levels, always and without even the slightest reservation, pass the debt that they, through reckless and corrupt spending practices created, penalties and all, on to future generations of Americans. Of course, if our nation doesn't turn itself around and soon, only those who are fortunate enough to still have jobs will feel the effects.

In the end, the bill always comes due, and as the ole timers used to say, "You always have to pay the piper," or as best described when referring to the China/America faith-based trade connection, "The devil always gets his due." One hard fact of life that all of us as consumers have reluctantly accepted comes in the form of the extremely high interest rates levied by lending institutions. In Joe's case, his inability to repay could mean bankruptcy. But when describing the same situation as it applies to our nation or what used to be our nation, it could mean the termination of its ability to borrow funds for future needs. This could result in the shutdown of government agencies or a complete collapse of a nation's government. But not to worry: I'm sure the Senate, Congress, and all necessary personnel working at the White House will never see an interruption in their pay. Isn't it amazing, not to mention unfortunate, that those in government who are the most responsible for the social and economic conditions they alone have created never feel the pain of their actions? While we the people are feeling the pain they're busy passing legislation that will give each and every single one of them another well-undeserved pay raise.

OK, Joe's a goner; there's nothing left for him but bankruptcy, and a complete meltdown, after which he'll face years and years of trying to rebuild his credit. But there's a brighter side for the government. This brighter side or last option, however, does not benefit people like Joe and the American middle class. As long as the debtor nation of America keeps paying the piper, even if it means by way of selling our nuclear technology, our ports, not to forget to mention our vital infrastructure or by way of signing special trade deals that take away millions more of American jobs, whatever has to be done, whatever it takes, rest assured that the corporate-owned politicians of this country will do anything to keep "the only game in town" going, at least for as long as China and the other lenders find it advantageous for themselves to allow it to do so.

Of course, nothing in life is perfect, and in all situations that deal with borrowing, even for a government, eventually, one way or another, the outcome will be a negative, and the brunt of it, as always, will come crashing down upon the shoulders of the taxpayers who pay the bills of incompetent, corrupt leadership.

Leona Helmsley once referred to us as "the little people." Well, for the little people, it means the continued loss of more and more jobs, the continued reduction in wages. Forget the benefits; they're long gone. As I mentioned in a previous chapter it will also mean the continued growth of what eventually will be the largest sector in American society. I'm referring to the working poor. Other things that go without question have already and will continue to occur, like allowing unsafe products to be sold on the American market. Deaths resulting from consuming poisonous food products will increase. The possibility of an eventual rise in a number of serious diseases including cancer and deaths resulting from them will add even more healthcare costs for an uncaring government that is already buckling under the skyrocketing costs of Medicare and Medicaid.

Thank God the politicians in Washington long ago voted in their own healthcare plan, a plan that we the voters have to pay for even though millions of us can't afford one ourselves.

Just like the credit card company that now has Joe as a regular customer and also by the proverbial balls, China now has America. Gee, Joe and our government have at least one thing in common. Someone has their hooks deeply imbedded in that oh so very sensitive area, a place that when squeezed will make both scream out in pain. Oh! Let me correct the last part of my previous sentence. If anyone screams out in pain, it's always the people who pay for the incompetence that for decades has run rampant in American government.

Getting back to G.W., the Bush administration can't afford to say no to China and Joe can't afford to say no to the credit card people. We already know who has America and Joe where they want them, and I guess we also know who is dictating America's trade agreements with China? Since our current situation with the most industrialized nation in the world is as it is, we can't honestly describe them as agreements. So I'd like to replace the word agreements with the word "terms," terms that are being dictated by China and I imagine, to at least some degree, buy all the other lenders. Our present day situation, at least as it concerns America. As I mentioned before has come about because of the extremely high level of corruption within past and most notably this current administration, administrations that for years have been living way beyond our ability to repay.

They can tell the American people about increased tax revenues and fast-paced deficit reductions till the cows come home. If indeed the deficit is being reduced, which is highly unlikely, it's at the expense of American jobs. As far as the Bush administration's being truthful about their claims of prosperity. If they are, it would be the first time since they came to power. Think about it. How can it be possible to have increased tax revenues when at the same time we've lost millions upon millions of American jobs, when wages and benefits continue to decline, when illegal aliens who do not pay taxes are replacing American taxpayers by the millions and to top it off, stuffing billions of taxpayer dollars down a toilet known as the Iraq war, and into the bank accounts of Halliburton and associates? There's only a couple of ways this could be even remotely possible. First of all, if the amount of tax revenue realized from all imported goods, which would include the tax on profits and sales tax, were greater than the taxes received from the wages of American workers who no longer have jobs relating to those products. The only other way it could be conceivably possible although only on the surface would be through the use of what Enron referred to as creative or innovative bookkeeping; in laymen's terms, cooking the books. I find myself leaning toward the kitchen method. Of course, only through a tremendous reduction in spending along with explanation number one would produce any sort of positive result, and since a reduction in spending is not going to happen, I have to conclude that the Bush administration's touting of a reduced deficit is just one more fabrication, which is a nicer word than lie.

When any nation has to depend on other nations including its enemies in order to keep its government afloat, they, like our friend Joe, will eventually find themselves standing on the slippery edge of a very dark abyss. In the end, those who have created the disaster that somewhere in the not-too-distant future surely awaits America will pack their bags and leave town. One or two of them might even retire to a ranch in Texas, or maybe Mexico; that is, unless by that time the United States has already become part of the grand North America borderless continent called the North America alliance of states. In that case, there might not be a Texas. It might be called state number 20 or G.W. Place; who knows.

One thing all politicians have in common besides not being able to tell the truth is that they all pray the ax won't fall until they're long gone from public office. Once they're clear of the mess they've created, they can proclaim to the American people that THEY ALONE WERE THE SINGLE VOICE IN THE NIGHT THAT CALLED OUT AND STOOD AGAINST THE VERY LEGISLATION THAT HAS CAUSED THE MESS WE NOW HAVE TO DEAL WITH. Whenever they say we, of course they're referring to us. And of course, he or she will make it well known that they gave it his or her all and we'll probably hear it in a statement that goes something like this. "BUT GEE! I WAS ONLY ONE VOICE AMONG MANY, AND YOU KNOW YOU CAN'T FIGHT CITY HALL." Oh, they have dozens of sayings and excuses, reasons for their failure to represent the will of the voting majority. I have only two words in reply: "BULL SHIT!" And you can quote me on that.

If the same situation were to have taken place in a small town, somewhere in west Texas, let's say about two hundred years ago, I do believe the individual at the center of all the attention would either be hung right on the spot by a very unhappy crowd of local citizens or if he or she were fortunate enough to be punished by townspeople who felt some degree of mercy, they would shortly find themselves wearing a suit made of tar and feathers. I suppose being run out of town on a rail was optional and depended on having a rail and a length of rope close at hand.

I had to phrase it as he, she, him, or her, so as not to offend the weaker sex. Who are in reality are definitely the stronger. The only mistake they made was in not organizing. If they had, they'd have been in the White House years ago. I'd like to state right now that I stand strongly behind equal rights for both men and women. As far as I'm concerned women have just as much right to get hung or tarred and feathered as men do, because out there, even today, there are people of both sexes who are in dire need of it. You know, they really used to do that. But that was back when Americans were uncivilized; back when people didn't put up with any crap; back when they could spot a carpetbagger on sight or by smell. Just think! If things were the same today, chances are George W. Bush might never have made it out of Texas let alone to the White House. Of course, being raised during those times, maybe just maybe he'd have developed a true compassion for the general population, compassion that, as I see it, he does not now possess. He might even have a few good feelings for his neighbors; then again, maybe not. I've found that as a rule, the longer I've live next door to people, the more likely I'd have less compassion for them, and the more likely I'd like to see less of them. Oh, and by the way, save whatever compassion you have for the poor working people. As far as I'm concerned, the rich don't need it, and those who are rich and could use it don't deserve it.

Time and time again, I've heard people exclaim, "These politicians are dumb, stupid," and many other adjectives that I'm not sure how to spell, so I won't use them. I have to confess that I too am also guilty of the same. I might even have used certain unflattering adjectives at one or more places in previous pages. But if they're as dumb as we think they are, how come things always work out to their benefit and never to ours? This being the case, I'm inclined to conclude that those who believe this and refer to them as such are really the dummies. Believe me, people, every move they make is calculated and designed to bring about the following results: first, to increase their own financial wealth; second, to increase the power and profits of the major corporations who have purchased their undying support not to mention their souls by contributing to them in one way or another; and third, to ensure the strength of their political party in order to successfully win elections. Oh, did I forget to include the security and welfare of America and its people? No, I didn't forget. That's not on their list. I'd like to make a comment concerning a candidate and candidates successful bid to office. Once in, once all the hoopla dies down, once the gala celebrations are over. These dedicated representatives of the people toss aside the speeches and all the promises that allowed them to successfully deceive the American people, and call their corporate supporters for orders pertaining to future legislation.

Because the following statement is central to the writing of this story I have to keep driving this point across. Every action, every piece of legislation passed over many years by these individuals who are suppose to represent us, but in reality, do not, has put America on the road to eventual destruction. It has caused a good majority of the rest of the world to turn away from us at a time when new and serious threats to our survival have begun taking shape, at a time when America needs friends and allies the most. Our self described leaders have turned us into a nation without friends, a nation that cannot exist without borrowing money from other nations, our enemies included. The last nearly eight years with a president who believes he's a king, and not an elected official has greatly affected our position as a world leader, and I truly believe that his actions have also greatly accelerated the rate of our nation's decline. The anti-American trade agreements created by past and present Administrations, has brought this once proud and independent nation to its knees. Because, of their seemingly limitless number of pork barrel projects, and their complete, and undying support for corporate and special interests. We can no longer afford to field a military that is up to the task of safeguarding America. The term "homeland security", as one 2008 presidential candidates stated, "is nothing more than a bumper sticker" is I believe a statement that is not so very far from the truth. Its creation being just one more department in a government bureaucracy that grows larger every day and probably is headed not by qualified individuals, but by people George W. Bush and/or Dick Cheney owe political favors to. This administration, more than any I've ever seen in my lifetime, has used lies, deception, and half truths in order to successfully plunder the taxpayers' dollars in order to fill the bottomless pockets of companies like Halliburton and its subsidiaries. Its place in history if accurately and honestly recorded will recall a president and an administration whose deeds costs the lives of thousands in a war based on lies. The only other legacy deserving of the Bush administration is the recognition of having successfully pulled off the largest bank heist in the history of mankind. They were able to accomplish this feat by using

Iraq as the excuse they had to use in order to justify the misappropriation of such a large amount of money.

Over the years, we've seen actors who became senators, governors, and even a president. I've always wondered if a politician took on the role of an actor, or if actors take on the role of politicians, or maybe they just continued in the role they've always played with only two substantial differences, that being the name at the top of their paychecks and the scripts they obliging read from, which are now written by a team of writers, employed by the most powerful companies in corporate America. Granted, the basic pay for people in politics isn't earthshaking, but by God, the extras are out of this world! One more question has puzzled me substantially. Do they learn to lie before being elected or just pick it up afterwards? Could be that it just comes naturally? After all, most of them do it real well. I wonder, do you think they hone their art? Maybe they practice those all-important, deceiving facial expressions over and over in front of the bathroom mirror each morning. And let's not forget that surprised look. You never know when they'll need it. Like when they're confronted by FBI agents who've just found $90,000 in their freezer. Occasions like that. These questions remind me of the age-old question, "Which came first, the chicken or the egg?" Whether we're talking about chickens or politicians I guess it really doesn't matter, because the fact is that they did, they are, and they do.

CHAPTER EIGHT

The Takers

Ever since man began walking upright and quite possibly even before, two separate groups or types of human beings became quite evident. I refer to them as "the givers and the takers." The givers, always bending to the will of the stronger, always gave, while the takers, always wanting more, always took. Whether it was more food, more and better weapons, a bigger cave, or the best-looking female or females in the tribe, they had that unquenchable desire for more. Using physical force, the strongest male dominated the group, and as long as he remained the strongest physically, he remained the leader. Any and all who disagreed with his decisions would be killed, beaten, or driven off. During the early days of man, his methods of domination and absolute control mirrored that of the wild animals that roamed our planet.

As time went by and man's thought processes continued to become more and more complex and his intelligence grew, a new kind of leader emerged. This individual wasn't the strongest physically, but in terms of intelligence, he was twenty miles ahead of his peers. This new breed of leader found that by using his intelligence, through reasoning, bribery, and sometimes a bit of extortion, which pretty much describes modern-day politics, he could enlist the aid of others who were physically stronger than he and more than willing, at least for a price, to carry out his bidding. Now, although not being physically able to directly confront and successfully dominate the other members of his tribe, group, village, or whatever, he could still assume his place of power as undisputable leader.

Although thousands of years have passed and man's intelligence, technology, and methods have progressed to a level prehistoric man could never even have imagined, the basic psychological makeup of today's man, especially our modern-day politician, has not progressed all that very far. If anything can be said of modern man, I suppose it would have to be that he's been able to successfully perfect one of his most basic undesirable character traits, the ability to lie and make others believe it. This ability has been raised to a level that can only be described as an art form. Oh, I nearly forgot. There's one more achievement that he should be extremely proud of, that being the title "the most dangerous animal on the face of the planet." There's no difference at all between the instincts that motivated early man and the instincts of those who lead today's nations, except one, that being the magnitude of the destruction he is now capable of. I believe the most current case in point is the war in Iraq, a war I will always believe was initiated with no intention of winning, and as such, a war that will not be won, but a war that was entered into for several reasons, none of which has anything to do with WMDs, freedom, or democracy. How about an outpost or maybe a stronghold in the Middle East, or how about profit? How does control of the Iraqi oil fields sound? Ever since the first crusade foreign powers have invaded and conquered the Middle East. But till this very day not one has been able to win. Not one has ever remained. America has won the war but they will never conquer the people. They will never change the people's beliefs or their way of life. And just as the armies that came before them, they too will leave.

I realize that I've stated this opinion more than once in prior pages. But I cannot stress it enough. Our lives today, along with the working class's deteriorating standard of living, are the results of years and years of corruption that has been allowed to go unchecked. The majority of the blame for our current situation rests solely upon the shoulders of those we elected to represent us. But the rest of the blame is ours.

Can we change the downhill out-of-control spiral that in recent years can almost entirely be attributed to corporate-dictated policies passed into law by what has to be the most corrupt administration this nation has ever seen, policies that by now have removed any doubt as to whom George W. Bush, Dick Cheney, and the Republican Party truly represent? I'm not at all confident that the American people can or will do what it would take to end

America's fall. But right now, I'd like to ask you the reader the following questions.

1. Will we the people survive the government-supported, corporate policies that have weakened our Constitution to the point of making it merely a nice old, ineffective, almost worthless piece of paper?

2. Make no mistake. I believe that our time, America's time, is running out. Can we change the course of limitless greed that corporate America has charted for us, or is it already too late?

3. What options do we have? And are we willing to implement those options?

4. Are we willing to make the sacrifices necessary to bring about that change, the change this nation's working class has to make in order for it to survive?

5. Once in power, will the Democratic Party spearhead that change? Nancy Pelossi's actions, along with the actions, or better said, inactions of the now democratically controlled Congress have pretty much destroyed any hope the American people might have had.

6. Should we begin looking at and supporting a third party? If we do successfully elect a party

outside the mainstream. Will its makeup consist of ex-Republican and Democratic Party members? Individuals who would bring with them the same corruption, big-money interests, and corporate-initiated policies that they have always represented? If in fact this situation were to occur, the same problems we're trying to escape would only follow. Because of the two-party political system we have today, whether we elect a Democrat or a Republican to any political office, one fact is and will remain absolute: If radical and positive change does not occur, and soon, as hard as it may be for us to believe or accept, if America's course remains unchanged, the United States, led by politicians representing national and international corporate interests, and without the support of the American people will some day be able to successfully dissolve America's borders. At that time, whether we like it or not. We will be forced to become citizens of an already partially constructed corporate world known as the Alliance of North American States. When that day arrives, America will no longer exist, and the quality of life for all Americans will only become much worse.

I keep asking myself. How has America's government become so corrupt and so uncaring for the voters who elected them? I sincerely believe that for years now the voters of this nation have been praying for a savior of sorts, an individual who loves his or her country and believes in honor, integrity and loyalty to the American people, someone, who would at last put the best interests of the America people ahead of those of corporate entities, and, special interests groups. Well, if such a person does exist. He or she hasn't stepped forward and by my way of thinking, never will. Through more presidential elections than I care to remember. We've heard the promises of change, and admittedly, they have always delivered on that promise. But unfortunately, especially during the Clinton, and Bush administration's time in office ninety-nine point nine percent of the changes we've seen have only been of a positive nature for minority groups, illegal aliens, and large national and international corporations. Not once, to any noticeable degree, have any of these changes benefited the two segments of our society that need help the most. I'm referring to working lower and middle class Americans.

After years of observation it's become clearly apparent, at least to me. That the men and women we've elected to political office have used the legislative power of their positions. To pass laws that has successfully enabled them to set themselves so far apart from their constituents. That they no longer feel obligated to represent the will of the voters who elected them to office. They feel no shame or regret when ignoring the demands of the voters in favor of the interests of national and international corporations. Once elected to office they immediately became part of the problem instead of part of the solution.

I believe one of the best examples showing how corporate America has for decades been able to control the outcome of our Presidential elections can be found by examining our extremely flawed election process. As most of us know the president of the United State is "NOT" elected by the American people. Oh, they try their best to make us believe that he is. But in reality, there are two groups who determine the final outcome of all our presidential elections.

The first group referred to as the Electoral College consists of 538 delegates. The second and entirely separate group, commonly known as Super Delegates is made up of hundreds of past and present elected officials, including past presidents. These two groups consist entirely of career politicians who owe their political lively hoods to the corporations who for years have donated, sometimes heavily, to their campaigns. They and they alone decide which candidates will represent America's two mainstream political parties and eventually occupy the Oval office. Oh, I've heard supporters of the process exclaim that each one of these delegates cast their vote the way the majority of the voters in their respective districts, through their election totals tells them to vote. This is generally true. But on several past occasions they have voted just the opposite. Probably in favor of the candidate that corporate America believed would work more closely with them. The history of American presidential politics has on more than one occasion, the last being the election of 2000, recorded a presidential election victory that went to a candidate who did not win by the popular vote.

Let's look at the whole process in a nutshell. Corporations, always trying to hedge their bets, always contribute to both the democratic and the republican presidential candidates. As I mention, the politically appointed or politically elected delegates actually decide the winners of each party's primary and the upcoming presidential election. I also mentioned. But will mention again. In many states, the delegates can vote their conscience rather than with the majority vote. Have you ever heard of a politician with a conscience? I've also been told that no matter what election we're talking about. Instead of counting all the votes cast in a district. At some point during the night, a sampling is taken and that determines the winner in that district. A case in point occurred during the 2008 state by state primaries when one state closed its poles early even though thousands of registered voters still hadn't voted. Also, how many times has an election been over and the results certified. When the following morning you watched a news report telling about thousands of absentee ballots that were still out? If we total up all the factors I've just mentioned. Who do you honestly believe chooses the leader of this country? Does the responsibility of electing a president fall entirely upon the shoulders of the men and women who cast their votes on Election Day? Or, does the true power to elect lay entirely in the hands of the financial backers who appear to have an endless supply of ready and waiting campaign contributions?

CHAPTER NINE

Corporate America's Creation
of the "Me Society"

I truly believe that society as a whole does not realize to just what extent corporate America's policies have affected the lives of each and every one of us. I also believe that corporate America uses and for many years has used, as a matter of policy, the same profit-driven methods that have served them so well. Policies, also used in order to control and manipulate society, as well as the American labor market. In plain and simple language, they have learned to use our most fundamental characteristics to their own advantage, the very same basic emotions that have enabled them to prosper to the extent that they have today. The trait or emotion I'm referring to and have mentioned numerous times in previous chapters is called "greed." Through the elimination of jobs and the continued reduction in wages and benefits, corporations throughout this country have been able to intensify and make more prominent than ever what I call the survival factor. Every human being's natural determination to survive, spurred on by corporate-profit-oriented policies have put workplace competition at a higher level than ever before. The results of these policies can not only be seen in the workplace but are increasingly noticeable in today's society. Increased job stress can be attributed to many of our current medical and social problems including high blood pressure, heart attacks, impotency and even suicide. Not to mention America's extremely high percentage of divorce, infidelity, road rage, robberies, murders, just to name a few. People who are basically honest find themselves so far in debt that out of desperation they sometimes turn to crime. America, because of the stressful times we live in has become a society of growing unrest and increasing turbulence.

With the closing of plant after plant, only to reopen in places like China, Japan, and Mexico, in conjunction with the exportation of millions upon millions of American jobs helped along by federal and in some cases state government policies that support the importation of illegal aliens, mostly from Mexico. Has successfully allowed American corporations to reduce their dependence on American labor to a point that now more than ever before allows them to pick and choose from a labor pool that is overflowing with potential workers, and just think, the Bush comprehensive immigration plan hasn't passed into law yet. Because of this, and the fact that today's average American worker has very little if any job protection in the workplace. We are now seeing people, some with college-level educations, being forced to compete in some cases for the most menial of jobs.

Corporate America, utilizing their cost cutting methods in order to achieve maximum profit, has over time created in this country an ever-growing and potentially dangerous labor and social situation, the effects of which, as I mentioned, we are seeing more and more everyday. Today, because of the passage of new legislation, legislation that most times results in the weakening of our labor laws in combination with ever-growing access to cheap labor. We are finding ourselves at the mercy of companies who only see profit and are totally devoid of loyalty to their country and its people. The current situation, which they intentionally created, has forced us to compete at a very stressful level with the people who work alongside us. I believe that competition is a healthy and necessary part of business. Without it, profits would suffer. But too much of anything, has always proven to be harmful. And as I stated, the extremely competitive atmosphere in today's workplace has created a very harmful situation.

This high-stress, competitive job market is I believe evident at least to some degree throughout every part of America. And in one way or another touches every one of us. These days, it's not about that promotion; it's about keeping your job. It's about finding that extra part-time job in order to maintain your standard of living. It's about putting food on the table and keeping a roof over your family's head. All these things, while the costs of basic necessities keep rising at a record-breaking pace. This is where the "me factor" comes in. "Screw the other guy." Fair play, friendship, and loyalty are now all but completely absent in the workplace. Anything and everything goes, no holds barred. Be careful what you say to another employee. It could very well cost you your job. You have to produce, and each year the bar is raised higher. So in order to survive, it instinctively becomes all about you and your family, it has to. Thanks to programs designed and brought to you by corporate America. The "ME" fixation or state of mind is here. And unfortunately for all of us, it doesn't stay at work. It climbs in the car with us. It rides along with us on the interstate. It goes home with us. It's with us twenty-four hours a day, seven days a week. Thanks to corporate America's cultivation of man's primal instinct to survive. We have now become a nation of me-first, me-last, and me-always people. We're so conditioned to achieve that we eagerly push the envelope every day. Beginning with the moment we climb in our cars. We go like hell from A to B in order to arrive, sometimes only seconds earlier than we would have if we drove at the posted speed limit. We're so determined to beat the other driver that it kills us to allow someone to change lanes in front of us. We're compelled to cut off another motorist for no reason other than that we're psychologically programmed to do so, and if you were to ask a driver why, you'd probably receive a reply like "screw 'um!" That, without a doubt, is the reply of a one hundred percent, dyed-in-the-wool "ME" person. Better stay clear, they're one step away from killing the next person who gets in their way. How about, "I don't know," or, "I just wanted to." How about this old standby? An excuse that always makes us feel justified, "He cut me off first." Each one of these reasons sound more like something a three-year-old would say rather than an adult, if there's really such a thing.

More and more we see people trying to get ahead of someone else, whether on the road or at the supermarket check-out. It's almost as if the average American begins each day by sticking a score card in his or her pocket. When they arrive home at night they total up all the points in order to determine whether or not they had a good day. The game goes something like this: In order to score we have to beat someone out of something or cause an inconvenience to someone else. You know, like making them wait for the parking place you're sitting in. The longer you make them wait, the more points you rack up pretty simple, right? These acts I've mentioned may bring a smile to your face, unless, that is, you're the driver waiting for the parking spot or the one who nearly demolishes his or her car when they're cut off by Mr. or Ms. Me. But the underlying reasons behind why we are so compelled to commit these acts are much more complicated and also much more serious. Thanks to corporate America, we've evolved into a nation where consideration for others has become increasingly rare, and winning at any cost is everything. Let's face it folks. Madonna isn't the only material girl. Americans in general worship material things. And anyone who picks up newspaper knows that there are quite a few men and women out there who will do anything, including murder, to get them. Take it from a guy who's been down the material road. In my younger days I worked my butt of and had all the toys. Eventually, instead of me owning the toys, the toys owned me. And that old saying "the best things in life are free." It's true. Modern day society more than ever before has become a society of individuals with very limited tunnel vision. They've been forced to look straight ahead keeping both their eyes on the ball. They haven't the time or the desire to consider others. They're too busy trying to survive in a world of ME people.

Crime is on the rise. Home invasions are increasing and becoming so commonplace that eventually, if they haven't already, they will soon be considered just a normal everyday occurrence. Or the price we have to pay in order to live in our modern-day society. As I mentioned in a previous chapter, it's a proven fact that as more and more people find it harder to make ends meet or become unemployed, the higher the crime rate will climb.

Now, let's discuss another facet of the corporate controlled ME society. Today, we no longer tell America's corporate sector what we want or would like. Through advertising campaigns costing millions of dollars they now tell us what we want. America's movie industry, by producing films like *The Terminator* rather than those stressing ethical family value's, has through the years been able to mentally condition generations of Americans. The end result has amounted to the same as telling society, especially the young people, that violence is OK, violence is neat, violence, is acceptable. If the dream factory in Hollywood can be credited with anything, I'd have to say that it would be the desensitizing of four or five generations of young people and because of it, today's society in general.

Corporate America's regular use of marketing firms, which as I mentioned before, are more or less just another term for think tanks, provides the findings. Then corporations use these what for most of us would appear to be unconnected, trivial bits and pieces of information in order to create their ad campaigns. At the same time continually injecting their own ideas of morality, and what they want us to want. If done correctly, and repeatedly. It will allow them to achieve their objective, which is to persuade the consumer to watch the movies they want them to watch and buy the products they want all of us to buy. At the same time, moving society's tastes and desires in the direction they want it to go. As I mentioned previously the same methods are used and used very successfully in politics. More times than not, if correctly applied, they can result in a successful election victory.

After the 2004 presidential election, George W. Bush kept speaking of all the political capital he possessed. He wasn't joking. That political capital made possible by the financial backing of corporate America. Cost the taxpayers much more than they ever dreamed of.

Let's move away from G.W. and his political capital, and for a moment, back to further discussion of another very powerful media tool. I'm referring to television and radio. Both are dominated by American business. Advertising, no matter what method is used, is designed to persuade the potential buyer to buy into a concept or belief, whether it relates to purchasing a company's product or supporting someone's political campaign. Through the very careful positioning of just the right word or words an advertisement can create an almost subliminal message. And when the listener is exposed to it repeatedly, it will affect how he or she perceives a product, a movement, proposed legislation, and yes, even a political candidate.

Today, corporate America is able to enter just about every facet of our daily life. What we watch on television, especially when exposed to the same type of programming over and over. It has a tendency to reshape how we think, act, or react to the events happening in the world around us. The information we receive, true or untrue, determines our likes and dislikes: everything we eat, how safe we feel the quality and safety of our food is; the design or style of the clothes we wear; the home we'd like to buy; the type of car we dream of someday owning; even what type of sexual acts we believe we must have in order to achieve personal sexual gratification. Through manipulative advertising practices based on and formulated with the use of psychology; a science that in part deals with and analyzes how we will react to certain words, pictures and experiences. They, not us, are able to dictate our tastes, our wants, and yes, even our desires. Sex sells big time. Why? Would it be such a dominant factor in today's society if we were not exposed to and given such huge daily doses of it? For years the entertainment industry has appealed to this primal instinct. Our desire or need for sex. Is there any relationship between how Hollywood portrays sex and violence, and the ever-increasing crimes of rape, torture, and murder?

Right now, you're probably saying to yourself, this guys nuts, or, "They don't control me. I can change the channel at any time." You're right, but why don't you? And if you do will watching another channel allow you to escape from the very same type of programming that you're trying to avoid? You can also turn off the boob tube. But studies have shown that chances are you won't. Why, is the majority of the subject matter portrayed on television and in the movies so much the same? The answer is simple. No matter what station you're watching. That program and all programs are created by people who wouldn't be able to market them without a sponsor. The sponsor wouldn't support them unless the programs they create conveyed the kind of message or messages, a company or organization wanted it to convey. All the things I've discussed, even though some may appear to be completely unrelated to the main theme of my book. In truth, are related. Over the years, the continued implementation of all of these things has brought about the creation of today's modern day American society. Including the political, economic and social situations we are now burdened with.

I'm afraid we're all pretty much trapped into conforming. At least to some degree, to whatever corporate America would like us to conform to. Has their domination of our lives been a positive factor? Take a good look around and assess what you see. Do you like the social, economic, and moral direction that Washington, AKA corporate America has chosen for us? When's the last time you voted for a candidate because you believed in him or her? Or was your vote given to the one you believed to be the better of two evils? No matter whom we vote for. The end game is, and will always continue to be the same. As long as corporate America has millions of dollars set aside to bribe politicians. As long as they continue to send lobbyists by the thousands to Capitol Hill, as long as man is as he is. The only thing we the people can do through the election process is change the names of the players. What we are powerless to do is change is the name of the game.

Will the end of the Bush administration in 2008 mean the end of corporate America's dominance, and advance toward their final solution? Their decades-old plan that today is within sight of being complete? No, not hardly. Now, just months away from the upcoming presidential election corporate America, along with special interest groups, having realized, that they have achieved as much as they possibly can, by financially supporting the Bush administration. Have left the dying carcass of the GOP and climbed aboard a fresh mount. One we all recognize as the Democratic Party. A party, which today, is merely an offshoot of the GOP. I'm sure corporate America realizes that although slim. There's still a chance of seeing another republican administration after 2008. It all depends on just how much the American people dislike the candidate fielded by the Democratic Party. I believe the majority of Americans, especially the older ones. Have long ago given up on supporting a candidate they believe in. How can we, when both are never any damn good? So, every four years we try to pick the best no good son of a bitch of the two. This time around, like the last two. There isn't one. At present, Hillary Clinton, and John McCain have raked in the most. Never fear America. The day after the swearing in ceremony of our next quote unquote leader, on that day, payback will once again begin. And the age old game of politics will continue on, just as it has for so many years. Maybe just a little bit slower at first. But still continuing on, as America's only game in town.

Conclusion

At over sixty years of age. Like most people who have been fortunate enough to live as long. I've arrived at a great number of conclusions and beliefs that at least in my mind, are set in stone. Here are just a few.

Biologically speaking, man is not only an animal. He's the most dangerous animal to ever walk the face of the Earth. Each and every day he has to exert his or her power and dominance over others. Whether on Capitol Hill, in the White House, or at the lowest but so very powerful and greatly overlooked level of government. One we all know to as our local county commission. After years of observing man's unstoppable drive to dominate others. Not only on a massive scale. But also on an individual and personal level; when coupled with the awful reality of knowing that our present-day global society has become so highly technologically advanced especially in the field dealing with mass destruction. And realizing the ease at which his most deadly creations can now be procured. I cannot help but believe his ultimate demise lies somewhere in the not-too-distant future.

Unlike his early ancestors today's modern man. Instead of being clothed in the skin of a woolly mammoth and carrying a large tree branch, or stone for defense. He now wears a three-piece suit. In place of a tree branch or stone he carries a cell phone, a brief case and a knowledge that enables him to destroy the world. Events I have witnessed throughout my life have led me to conclude that 99.9 percent of all tragedies that have occurred or will ever occur; whether large or small; whether happening in 1000 B.C. or 2008 A.D. Have come about because just as in the beginning. When the strongest male ruled a tribe of his peers, or today, when an individual or group of individuals rule a nation. Because someone wants more, more of something they have no legal or moral right to have more of.

From the very beginning, when the first human being hired another to perform some sort of task. There's been a certain level of strife, animosity, envy, or whatever between the two factions. As more people began hiring others to perform these tasks. It was inevitable that over time two separate groups would emerge to become opponents, or as in some cases, downright enemies. Throughout history, the factions of labor and management, whether here in the United States, or abroad, have carried on a never-ending struggle, a struggle that has pitted one against the other. Big business, not only trying to hold onto profits, but always, trying to find ways to increase them.

As an employee, you were either on the side of management or on the side of labor. You couldn't have it both ways. It wasn't long before the two teams began fighting it out tooth and nail, each trying to best the other at every turn. Looking at our job and wage situation today it isn't hard to see who's won the battle. It's been said that there are two things in life that are inevitable: death and taxes. I'd like to add labor disputes to that list. For as long as man exists, problems arising from this worker-management arrangement will also exist. Why? Because like I've mentioned previously, man is as he is, and always will be. Today's man, other than the fact that he's much more intelligent and thus much more lethal than his ancestors, hasn't changed at all.

The bottom line is this: Want positive change? We'll only see such change when the people we elect to represent "US" begin to care. When will they care? Most likely, on the morning after it's too late, too late for us.

"If there's one lesson that we the American people should have learned from the past seven-plus years of the Bush administration. "It should be just how fragile our way of life truly is."

D.A. Robinson

THE END ?

About the Author

I was born on June 16, 1947, in Troy, New York. Just across the river from the state capital of Albany and four blocks from School 12 and the then operational Republic Steel plant. Until I was eight my family lived in my grandfather's old wood frame, two story house. Near the top of an extremely steep, cobblestone hill, called Lincoln Ave. For years, my parents saved quarters, dimes, nicklels and pennies with the intention of leaving the city behind. Soon after my eighth birthday, we did just that. My father passed away when I was twelve. Shortly after, while attending Averill Park High. I began working at a local garage in the then small farming town of Poestenkill, New York. After graduation, I spent one year at a local community college before enlisting in the United States Army. Vietnam was going strong. And like many kids my age. I decided to serve my country. As fate would have it. I survived those three years and returned to the rural life I'd left behind. Since then, my life has mirrored most

Americans. It's held periods of prosperity and happiness as well as times of varied degrees of depression and hardship. As for writing credentials, I have none to speak of. Over the years I've had several opinion pieces published in various local Florida newspapers. The St. Petersburg Times being one of them. I'm not a celebrated scholar or a syndicated news columnist. I'm just an American who has a statement to make. Corporate America's Final Solution is that statement..

www.ingramcontent.com/pod-product-compliance
Lightning Source LLC
Chambersburg PA
CBHW020915290526
45784CB00002BA/559